M000167584

Praise for Carrie Lloyd

"Prude *is not worthy, pious, or preachy; it's truthful, it's flawed, and it's inspirational.*"

Malcolm Croft
Senior Editor at Carlton Books UK, freelance author, editor

"*Carrie Lloyd is Bridget Jones meets Ann Voskamp. I found her refreshing, insightful and encouraging.*"

Christianity Magazine

"*The Oxford English Dictionary defines 'prude' as a puritan, prig, killjoy, moralist, or informally, a 'Goody Two-shoes.' Carrie Lloyd's new book,* Prude: Misconceptions of a Neo-Virgin, *stands in fierce opposition to the OED's definition. Lloyd is an earthy, funny, insightful woman embarked on a most unusual journey. Having experienced the modern world's sexual 'liberation,' Lloyd makes the outlier's decision to forgo sex before marriage. No easy path, this, as we soon discover in the pages of* Prude. *From incredulous girlfriends, to damp and derailed boyfriends, Lloyd finds that 'holding out' is fraught with uncertainty and frustration. Faith helps her prevail, but that too is subject to doubt and redefinition.* Prude *is not a cenobite's memoir, but a romp through traditional church and modern bedroom, both of which are found to be leached of meaning and spiritually threadbare. Whatever you feel about faith and Christianity, meeting Carrie Lloyd in the pages of Prude will convince you of one thing: Chastity can be sexy.*"

Michael Braverman
Executive Producer, A Smith Company

"Carrie is brilliant because she's prepared to talk about the things that so many of us shy away from, or don't know how. In this funny, frank account of her own journey (which I suspect will be sneakily read by just as many men as women), she unpacks issues which are both timelessly relevant and culturally definitive, and gives a rare and candid perspective on everything from porn to self-sabotage. Prude is a sassy, poignant, hilarious and brilliantly-written story about what happens when a regular girl living at the heart of a sex-mad society, suddenly meets the God who redefines everything."

Martin Saunders
Contributing Editor at Christian Today

"Carrie's book is a MUST-read for every person committed to sexual purity who has struggled with sex, self worth, shame, and judgment while on the road to freedom and...Mr. Right. Prude is fresh, real, and honest in ways no other Christian authors are speaking today. Instead of being politically correct in terms of 'Christianese,' Carrie says it like it is so that women can actually be set free by dialogue they relate to."

Cynthia Garrett
Inspirational Speaker, Evangelist, Executive Producer,
and Host of The London Sessions on TBN

"Get ready to go on an journey with Carrie Lloyd in a real, raw and relevant adventure of what happens when you taste 'free love,' and then decide to save the gift of sex to be fully enjoyed the way it was designed!"

Tom Crandall
Youth Pastor of Awakening, Bethel Church, Redding

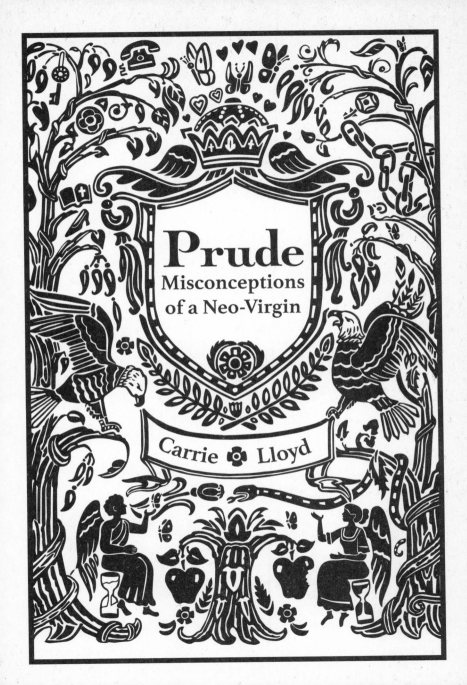

Prude
Misconceptions of a Neo-Virgin

Carrie ✿ Lloyd

Prude
Copyright © 2016 by Carrie Lloyd

Red Arrow Media
Redding, California

All rights reserved.

Cover Design: Rachel Cloyne with Pickled Ink
www.pickledink.com | @InkledPicks

Interior Design: Vision Tank, UK
www.visiontank.co.uk | @ visiontankuk

Author Photograph: Alex Douglas
@blaowphotography

Printed in the United States
redarrowmedia.com

For the two who held onto hope for my arrival after waiting so long.
For the two who introduced me to love, peace and light—my parents:
Rev. May Lloyd, and the late Dr. Rev. John Antony Lloyd.

Contents

Preface

Chapter 1   Forbidden Fruit...17

Chapter 2   Me and Margaret Thatcher.........................33

Chapter 3   Damned if You Do, Damned if You Don't.........45

Chapter 4   Coping or Copping Out?..............................61

Chapter 5   Covering Your Bases.....................................77

Chapter 6   The Conversation...89

Chapter 7   Daddy's Girl...101

Chapter 8   The Decadent Days.....................................115

Chapter 9   Make Love, Not Porn..................................133

Chapter 10   The "F" Word..147

Chapter 11   Poison in a Pint...159

Chapter 12   Worth the Wait?..173

Preface

Today people deny a belief in God more than ever before, and Christianity is too often represented by some clever clogs who directed a documentary on crazy nuts worshipping God and then setting themselves (or perhaps other people) alight moments later. The word God has been thrown around like a rolling stone for centuries. God has often been connected to maniacs, terrorists, pedophiles, racists, bigots, even scientologists. When people mention God, the response is equal to that of someone with vertigo about to plunge on a bungee rope. Perhaps, before we even go into talking about my life and the virgin years within, it's best to explain the version of God I mean before this book is thrown into the portal of hell itself.

Understandably, the audience participants might question the likes of someone like me who says she loves Jesus. I've been an atheist as well as a Christian. I've given every minister in England I could find a run for his or her money. I've contested time and time again in apologetics classes, in religious education classes, in Quaker meetings, on film sets, in Catholic churches, in Protestant churches, in Alcoholics Anonymous meetings, and even in hospice wards with those who said they visited Heaven. I questioned them all. And regardless of my beliefs—my horrific religious ones as a kid, my arrogant ones as an atheist—my findings came down to what we all searched for in the beginning. Before we were taught anything about God, before we could place pen to paper, we searched for a meaning. And this was my conclusion:

God is love.

Any exegetical attempt of scripture to suggest that God is not agape love, or that He was the one who placed an AK-47 in the hands of a seven-year-old boy is, for me, misguided. The essence, the force that joins people together, that purges a mother who lost her son to the IRA of unforgiveness, and the deeper need to do what is best, what is righteous, what is kind, what is humble, what is pure, what is beautiful, what gives instead of takes—that is God.

It is not as simple as some giant Abraham Lincoln sitting on a throne in the sky. To be as complex as we are leaves room to believe in, to at least question if there are similarities between our Creator and us. That we are able to love at all, to prefer another's life or happiness above our own, points to an inner wiring that goes against the natural desire for self-preservation, and this doesn't make sense without an original source of love. For me, that source didn't just create love. That source is love. And, as far as I'm concerned, love means more than affection. Love longs for, love desires. God being love therefore amalgamates a desire to have relationship with us. It is because of this that I call God a father and there is a union between God and me.

Though God is both female and male in form, I use the word Him for relativity, but not in accuracy. The complexities and multi-dimensions of God, the many facets that travel outside of space and time, the evolutionary components that built and formed the earth, the science, the mathematics, the quantum physics, the design itself is all God. The one whom C.S. Lewis and Tolkien discussed at length so often in The Eagle and Child pub in Oxford is the God I speak of in this book. I do believe God was incarnated into human form, and that Jesus wasn't "just a nice guy." I know plenty of nice guys. I doubt we'd be talking about any of them 2,000 years later.

So whenever God is mentioned, attempt to not bolt upright with walls or prejudice against something that should be seen as life-giving. I realize many of us have had our negative encounters with Christians: Some left a bad taste in our mouths, some tried to convert rather than let us speak, some wanted our souls instead of treasuring our hearts. But open your mind for a moment and trust there is no ulterior motive, no quest to do anything other than tell a story without a hidden agenda. Resist the urge to bring any preconception from any propaganda you've viewed in the press or on any television network. It's far greater than some poor behavior carried out by Man. Anything they did was not God's fault. After all, this is a free world, and for God to be love in any real way, He must also give us free will.

Think me not an idiot for believing in something beyond what we see, and we will get along just fine. Besides, it was not always this way for me; discovering such a God—one not of religion, of law, of restrictions—was all part of the journey, one I might have done differently had I the chance to write the story again.

CHAPTER 1

Forbidden Fruit

" Be honest, is being you awful? And what exactly is a *neo-virgin*?"
A fair question, one I get asked more times than I care to count.
This is the twenty-first century after all, the age of information overload,
global perspective and influence, universal exploration, technological and
scientific advancement, and creative freedom. We now have an expectation
to live a life full of toe-curling adventure and authentic self-expression.
Does not having sex before marriage help meet that agenda? It feels like the
opposite of being free, liberated, and unhindered. How could anyone
possibly have fun without it?

"I don't understand, Carrie, why would you not have sex when you've
already done it?" This question was posed by my friend Goldilocks at a
Christmas party two years ago.

"No one said this to Aileen Wuornos, did they? 'Well, if you've
murdered one guy you might as well keep going.'"

"What?" she asked, perturbed by my association of pre-marital sex to serial killing.

I revoked my statement. "It made sense to me."

This particular discussion was instigated by an event that had occurred a few days before. I met someone, let's call him "Montane," at a party. He was dazzling in all natures and met most of the "wants" on the checklist of ideals:

Tall—*quite*.

Dark and handsome—*yes*.

Kind and witty—*of course*.

Intense and curious—*abundantly*.

Highly influential and well known in his industry. The money itself didn't matter so much as the influence he could have—and did have—in the world.

It had only been three months since I had been dumped without much explanation by my ex-boyfriend on Facetime whilst he was travelling on a lads' holiday. When my non-Christian friends discovered that the ex was a thirty-something virgin, they deduced he must be gay—no man could wait that long for sex, and the large number of vest tops he owned seemed to confirm their suspicion. A trip to New York helped heal my hurt heart, and I returned to Scotland to a party nine hours north of my home in England.

Montane opened the front door and shared his condolences on hearing of my break up. "I heard he was gay?"

I looked to my friends John and Goldilocks in the background with an accusatory, *How many people have you told that my ex is gay* look. "Well, no. Not exactly—"

John interrupted in the background, giving a close inspection to some cutlery and shouting, "Do you think this spoon is bent?"

I attempted to continue explaining the real situation. "I think he just wasn't that into me. Apparently he didn't think he could meet my needs. Although when I asked what they actually were, he couldn't answer. The truth is that I made sure I had no needs. More the fool me."

John couldn't resist using another projected voice to tale end, "Darling, could you pass me the cushion thing, you know the poof from over there please?"

"I can assure you my virgin ex-boyfriend was straight."

John's smug grin shot across our way.

Montane showed a concerned smile.

As the night progressed, I found Montane more and more fascinating, surrounded by really interesting, quirky, expressive people. He told stories that had us gasping for breath, but he still came across as genuinely humble. Despite knowing how influential he was in the world, he wasn't afraid to listen to another opinion. He was a gentle giant, wrapped in the kind of power and gusto that made one's knees a little shaky.

We finally found ourselves alone when I bumped into him in a corridor. As he hugged me, I wished him a Happy Christmas. Then suddenly, a familiar whisper came to me, overriding my own thoughts: *Ask him about being known.* Oh God, not now. Now is not the time to get spiritual. But such was my stance that my relationship with God was stronger than my fear of looking crazy.

I held my breath and went for it. "Can I ask you something?"

"Sure?"

"Do you feel known?"

Silence. His face dropped, his eyes brightening as if I just told him he'd won his net worth all over again.

"That's an incredible question."

Someone bumped into him, and we were soon parted by a crowd of people all wanting to play Jenga. They called us to join them.

"Well, I just wondered." I tapped my heart.

He winked.

When we sat down to play, he positioned himself across from me. Throughout the game he kept glancing at me, placing blocks of wood without really looking and repeating again, "That's really an incredible question."

Once the game ended, I didn't see him for the rest of the evening, slipping off into the night without a word.

Two weeks later I received a text with a screen shot of text conversation from Montane to Goldilocks. It read: "I had a dream about your friend Carrie last night, I need her number."

I texted Goldilocks, "Does he know that I won't be doing anything physical with him?"

"Well, I told him that, but I also said that Jesus might just turn his head away so you can have a little flirt and tickle."

"You're the worst friend. Oh, dear Lord, help me."

"Yes, perhaps praying would be good. It's out of my hands." Goldilocks, although an atheist, thought she'd been helpful.

Truth was I adored this guy.

Within five minutes of receiving a text from Goldilocks, Montane was in his car, ready to drive down to England. And it wasn't to play another board game. There was something in my question that made him curious about me.

"I'm driving up to find you."

"But I'm nine hours away. You'd not be here until 10:00 p.m."

"10:00 p.m. it is."

"But you can't stay here. I live alone and...and...well you can't stay over."

I began texting my friends for an emergency meeting, seeking advice on how to resist this guy for whom I had every urge and feeling. I had abstained from sex for four years, but this was the greatest temptation to date. I also just happened to be writing about purity for an article when I got the call.

"I really appreciated his work with—" Montane was so influential, my friends kept coming back at me with their feedback on what he was known for.

"I'm not looking for Wikipedia results; I'm looking for help here, people!"

10:00 p.m. arrived, and there he was—hundreds of miles from his mansion, three inches away from my face.

"So this was a choice," I said. "A nice choice. But a choice."

"I know." In he came and poured himself some water. He scanned the room, my photos, a painting I had commissioned Francesca Lowe to paint called "Grace." Then he took a closer look, reading the scriptural context.

I was clearly nervous. Stunned that he came all this way, frightened to consider his expectations.

"God saved me a year ago," he stated quietly.

Oh no. I could have resisted so much easier if he had told me he doesn't believe in God.

We went on to talk for hours about how God saved him, about his past relationships, his friends, his family, and how when I fall in love with him I can move into his place in the middle of nowhere, the one that no one knows about. He brings up *Fraud*, a collection of essays by David Rackoff. I pick mine up from my coffee table. Every part of me was melting. I wondered what our wedding would be like. And then I charged myself not to be *that* type—you know, the deranged woman who writes her vows after one conversation.

His spontaneous eagerness was a refreshing touch compared to the fearful men I had dated before in the Church. We talked sex, and how wonderful it was, how I didn't do it anymore, holding out for my hero.

"Oh, so you really are waiting until marriage?" He seemed shocked.

Internally I wondered just how clear Goldilocks had been about Jesus and my reformed virginity.

"Did you think it was a coy remark, part of a cute branding strategy?"

He smiled, refreshed to have a "no" girl around him. He made another cup of tea, while I couldn't stop watching him.

2:00 a.m. and I had hit my limit, too tempted to have him around without an action I knew I'd regret. I shoved him out of the house in the nicest way possible and found him a hotel. No one in his life had probably carted him into a Holiday Inn, but here he was, waltzing into a room he had no intention of staying in alone. He looked at me with his deep, Labrador puppy eyes and with such exclusivity that I felt like he'd only ever looked at me like that in his life. I had to remind myself, *He does this all the time.*

3:00 a.m.—7:00 a.m., he slept.

I didn't. Mainly because I knew within a minute I could drive to his location.

This could be the start of a whirlwind romance. Then it wouldn't be a mistake. It would be love. Love is never a mistake. And love covers a multitude of sins—that's most probably biblical. And the Song of Solomon is a whole book of exuberant passion. Driving down from Scotland. I mean that's something.

Go. To. Sleep. Carrie. I stayed put under my duvet until sunrise. The sound of my phone startled me out of my half-conscious state. He was going home, which was a good thing for me, but I told him to wait for me to come over first. When I knocked on the door, he answered barely clothed, which didn't help my desire to pretend he was my husband for the morning.

"All I wanted was to fall in love with you and live with you at the place that no one knows about. Perhaps it's some location where you kill girls and keep their corpses upright whilst you watch television, but I'm going to go with my original assumption and believe it's the palace of dreams. Probably with a more exclusive playroom than Christian Grey, the difference between you and him being that you mentioned commitment last night."

He kept watching me ramble, smiling at my consternation.

"In short, I wasn't rejecting you because I said *no* to sex. I'm probably the only woman in your life to have ever declined it."

He smiled and grabbed me, pulling me into the room and shutting the door.

I snuggled into him and held onto him for as long as I could.

He wrapped his arms around me. "You seem happy," he whispered. "And I respect your values."

I had hope. Would he stay? Would he stay and build rapport, and then build a relationship, and then would sex be an ecstatic crescendo on our wedding night?

"But I'm going to need to have sex with my girlfriend."

Oh. The truth sunk into my red-hot, coursing blood like an injection of methanol.

"But I do respect your values. Should you ever change your mind though…"

I was conflicted. This couldn't really be unconditional love if he had this specific condition. And if this wasn't really love, then…this wasn't really what I wanted either.

In the middle of his display of comfort, a leaf blower started making a racket in the courtyard. Within a second, he burst into a comedy act, as the leaf-blower grew louder, sounding like it was about to come through the French doors.

"THEY'RE HERE!" Montane flung himself across the room, spreading himself against the doors. "The Christians are here to snatch you away! RUN FOR YOUR LIFE, CARRIE!"

I broke into a thousand hysterics. He picked me up the way I imagined he would when we crossed the threshold of the murder palace, and then he sat me on the bed.

"She can't hear you. I taped it all up down there four years ago." I held onto him for a little longer, pulled his chin up so his eyes could meet mine, kissed his cheek, and said, "I want to be a friend to you, a woman who doesn't want anything from you. Just friendship. Just conversation. Society killed the art of talking so long ago, and yet, it's where my heart ignited last night. You're fascinating. A true gent. I did all of this not to restrict you, but to honor you."

As I left the hotel, my tears felt like waterfalls. I walked away from a man I had only dreamt could exist, but couldn't really have. I returned to my empty flat, the scent of his cologne still lingering.

Goldilocks texted an hour after his departure: "Did he get in touch?"

"Did he get in touch?! Babe, he SHOWED UP!"

"WHAT?!?!?! You see, this is the difference between heterosexual men and homosexual men disguised as heterosexual men. They actually do something about wanting you. Did you…?"

"No, of course I didn't."

"Not even if Jesus turned away?"

"Remind me to explain Jesus to you one day so that this all might make sense."

Late night tears of not having the man I wanted in my life aside, I found a gorgeous joy in entertaining my friends with my abstinence adventures. Did I decide to stop having sex just for the pure comedic value? A topic of conversation? A man-tester to see who would still hang around after I didn't give in? Or was it to acquaint myself with the ability to manage freedom for the sake of not hurting others? There was a method to my sexless madness.

To fulfill our innate desires, whatever they were, we acted out, we strived, we consumed. Life was about the latest Apple product, Cirque du Soleil tickets, Instagrammed pictures at the Ice Hotel in Norway, swimming with Dotty the Dolphin, having 2.4 children with an additional one adopted on a Zimbabwean mission trip. We celebrated our Employee of the Month award at our local Soho House club, parading our membership card like it was security access for the UN. Consumption created our identity. We strove for status. We acted liberally, ensuring we were not so backward to support groups such as the radical extremists, but not too forward to welcome polyamory into our living room. Yet we never outwardly denied any form of "fetishy" activity either since it made us seem prudish.

No one wanted to be prudish.

To be such would confirm some rigidity of the self, creating some uncomfortable tension about being liberal or "free."

Everyone wanted to be free.

I chewed the forbidden fruit, but it didn't give back as much as it took. I decided to hang up my Agent Provocateur negligees, the contraceptive pill, and my need to perform for requited love. To my friends, this barbarity of returning back to purity at the age of thirty-one must have been catalyzed by fear, heartbreak, or a need to make penance, a flagellant-inspired shame.

"Perhaps it was that nun at St. Bueno's that time she went on an eight-day silent retreat?" they speculated.

My reasons had nothing to do with shame, a one-way ticket to hell, a hint of damnation, mortification of the flesh, or a German nun called Sister

Renate. It had a lot to do with a little life experience and a tangible desire to build my house on an emotionally mature rock, not a hotbed of quicksand.

What was the point of "saving myself" once more? An excellent question, and one not easily answered. What was the point of having sex (or not having sex) at all? It was a desire within, a pull toward connection, relationship, love. The world needed love. We needed love. The contradiction was that we had sex in the hope for love, while trying to believe that sex and love are two different things.

Virgins have never had a reputation of being fun, nor being very "grown up." They *did* have the reputation of attracting hostility, harassment, or just plain unkindness. Name-calling and jokes made even well into adulthood. In the same vein as mothers who tell childless women, "You don't know anything about life until you have children," so too had those who refused coital connections been belittled for their decision by those who chose to have sex.

Society's opinion of sexual purity certainly hasn't been helped by depictions of virgins in movies and on television. Watching virgin bride shows only resulted in me throwing my ESV Bible at the TV screen; you know, the ones with virgins who had been so pure in their romantic journey that they still hadn't had sex two years *after* marriage.

The idiots.

Camera crews followed a poor husband, taking a cold shower in case he should experience "naughty bedroom thoughts," while his wife would calm herself by eating a raw sweet potato. And so, others often categorized me as being part of the Sweet Potato Brigade–an association with which I had no intention of partnering.

On top of everything else, the word *chastity* has become distasteful to modern ears. The Millennial generation no longer wants to know about the bitter cup of abstinence. We have heard it for decades. We know the

statistics. We know that HPV can cause cervical cancer, that syphilis
is coming back with a vengeance, that an attachment hormone called
"oxytocin" becomes active in the system after sexual interaction, distorting
emotional rationale in choosing the perfect mate to wed.

We've heard the cautionary nightmares handed to us by our parents,
teachers, mentors, and, let's not forget, Saint Oprah. We watched the rise
in teenage pregnancy in the last two decades. We met the love-children of
those liberated Woodstock hippies. Well, those who hadn't fell prey to an
illegal abortion by some dodgy Harley Street doctor. A sixties wild-child
herself, one columnist wrote an article reflecting the era that was often
heralded as the period of sexual liberation (though I'd argue it was being
introduced much earlier than this):

> After a decade of sleeping around pretty indiscriminately,
> girls of the sixties eventually became fairly jaded about sex.
> It took me years to discover that continual sex with different
> partners is, with very few exceptions, joyless, uncomfortable and
> humiliating, and it's only now I'm older that I've discovered that
> one of the ingredients of a good sex life is, at the very least, a
> grain of affection between the two partners involved.

"A grain of affection," you say? I like her honesty. This was stated often
by my parents' generation. The sixties lovers never gained anything out of
it other than experimentation. When they found themselves at maturity,
most of them would not have repeated it again. After all, the sixties
revolution created free lust, not love. All lust had done was devalue the
power of sex.

But why was sex so forbidden before marriage in faith circles? Why
exactly did religious text tell us to hold out? It was a question that ran

from before the time I even knew what sex was to the years I chose to have sexual relationships in my twenties.

Here we are, aware of our sexual desires, aware of the realness of all that they are, yet unable to manage our desires in the greatest freedom culture to date. It's not that we shouldn't feel sexual, but we could manage it a whole lot better by understanding ourselves. This tale we all told each other, that sex and love could be separated, wasn't the human design I had learned first-hand or by dragging another girlfriend out from the gutter, crying because some guy didn't call. That wasn't *natural*. To detach the body from emotional feeling was as insane as saying, "Taking a swim in the ocean won't necessarily get you wet."

Just because current culture told me that I "should," didn't mean I needed to fall for the delusions the world around me told itself. Trends rarely cared for the sanctity of commitment, never mind marriage; they definitely didn't give a bride's garter for anyone's heart, really. Cultures changed constantly, but the body, the design and architecture invented many moons ago, always stayed the same.

The pull to want to be known, to be respected, honored, laughed with (and not at) required, in my experience, foundations, building blocks, and a collaboration of virtues that were built within the individual and then leaked into the relationship. Sex was a congratulatory reward for all you had fought for, not an entrée meal.

The real aim, the most natural desire for all of us is to love and be loved in return. Having sex didn't guarantee that for me or for my friends, especially when men had often checked out of the relationship quicker than checking into a random hotel room, leaving no forwarding address. The ambitious hope that we can have a wild night of passion and it not mean anything perhaps suits some men, but for most of us women, we want that grain of affection, and affection looks like more than a nine-hour drive. It looks like staying around, even if we just want to talk.

Call me an extremist, but I'm all about the commitment, accountability. For all the ball-and-chain stigma it's collected over the centuries, marriage is still the highest symbol of commitment to date.

Still, even some of my closest friends don't understand me. "But…but what *do* you do? What do you actually do if you can't have sex?"

"Crochet." My smile would always be met with utter disdain, as if they had been waiting for the final scene in the *Harry Potter* series and it all turned out to be a dream.

"Conversation. That moment when you say something and then they reply. That sort of thing. We'll hang with friends, eat s'mores around the fire. Discuss politics. Watch some awful movie about giant whales. Go clubbing and share the love of Christ to cokehead ravers. Two people can find plenty of things to do instead of dancing the horizontal tango."

When in conversation with my atheist, agnostic, humanist, Catholic, Presbyterian, Baptist, Muslim, Buddhist, Lutheran, Satanist (oh, all right, I don't have any Satanist friends), I find that we all want the same thing: to find a connection, to find kindness, to be a team, to create a purpose that means more than watching *Seinfeld* reruns and playing Rugby on the weekend, and to know beyond a doubt that I don't need to worry if he'll come home stinking of Chanel No. 5. I want sacrifice on the man's part instead of sacrificing myself all the time. I want a joy that finds me laughing at 2:00 a.m. on a park bench because we got locked out. I dream of the ability to be long-suffering when the times are tough, knowing the rough must be taken with the smooth.

I want trust before intimacy, peace before fear.

It's why I laugh when people tell me the Bible is out of date. I find it post-modern. In time, future generations may learn just how much we've hurt each other with sexual leniency. Will they see that the heart isn't as easily mended as we perhaps originally hoped?

Look at the beginning of the human story. Two people were given a choice: Take a bite from the Tree of Knowledge, or trust God and take a bite from the Tree of Life. Although sex made us all *feel* more knowledgeable, be it about ourselves or about someone else, it didn't necessarily bring us life. And ironically, the more I went on my journey, I found not biting the forbidden fruit more life-giving. In short, when nourishing from the Tree of Life, I became more knowledgeable about life itself.

So if I'm being honest, is being me truly awful?

As you delve into these stories, from virginity to my testing twenties, perhaps it's best for you to decide.

CHAPTER 2

Me and Margaret Thatcher

L et's not bother with the rather boring formative years, as everyone knows conversation and insight is a little ambiguous between the ages of zero to seven. But come 1988 the age of eight, harassment from some local schoolboys added a little color into my day and brought out the awesomeness in my Dad, a.k.a. "Pops."

"If you so much as breathe on my daughter or threaten to flush her head down the school toilet one more time, I will hunt your ear lobes down. I will drag you to your parents, if you're not already feral boys living in forests, and I will annihilate you with one blow of my tongue…in Christian love, of course."

Like all good fathers, Dad enjoyed protecting his girl by reading the Riot Act to a group of kids bullying me. I made a decent shield out of Dad's right leg when I was eight as he continued, "Are we all completely clear on the regulations moving forward?"

Their heads down, they mumbled, "Yes."

My dad's terrifying speech swiftly changed to: "Great! Come on, Kid." He tucked my head under his arm as we walked away, "Let's get you on that Ducati to brush off this escapade…do that walk you do, Carrie."

"What are you talking about?"

"You know, your strut walk that says, 'My dad's got my back.'"

"That's not a walk. There is no such walk."

"You're doing it now! That's it!"

"This is my regular walk, Dad. This is how I walk."

"That's my girl! But slow down, my leg is bad from shrapnel in the Second World War."

"Dad, you don't have a bad leg, nor were you in the Second World War."

"How would you know? You weren't even born."

"Yes and neither were you. Stop it, stop limping."

Our conversation faded out as we walked farther away from the village bullies accompanied by my father's asthmatic laughter. Aside from becoming a ninja warrior when I needed, he introduced me to ideologies where there were no limits, where righteousness was as necessary as oxygen, and where Lawrence Olivier's dulcet tones were the most stunning to grace Planet Earth. He taught me my value, and when men came into my life, he had an "approve or deny" regimen that never faltered, which manifested in such things as not speaking to a boyfriend if he had dishonored me. Dad kept a standard that I trusted. As a father, he loved me without ulterior motives.

Having no siblings meant I was only surrounded by adults at home. At the age of seven I could converse with them about mortgages and life insurance, and even my neighbors knew to be fully prepped to discuss my Sylvanian Families toy collection in case they should see me over the garden fence. I'd eagerly listen to my parents' musings on the FTSE and the government's welfare budget, and then bid adieu as I walked back into the living room, trying to remember where I had left Ken and Barbie. I celebrated my birthdays with two separate groups: one for the children pre-puberty (school friends) and one for those post-menopause (my parents' friends).

From an early start, I learned how to know my audience and picked the best of both worlds. I could be stupidly sword-fighting like the Musketeers with my little buddies, then finish my day inspired by the adults' driven vision, the missionaries who talked of saving a baby with a small syringe of hydrating salts and water. Adults weren't throwing around this desperate need to copulate with each other; they weren't trying to get stoned, nor did they find Beavis and Butthead amusing. They didn't get the jokes.

With my parents being Baptist ministers, I attended church, yet I did not have a relationship with a divine being who provided love or value in the same way as my father. I figured the universe must have flashed into being, and no one could find out what caused that one-hundred-thousand-million degree centigrade combustion. Yet the mathematical rules that sustained our existence, the laws of nature, creativity, the water that made up 80% of the earth, could not have been placed by something that didn't have the creation of a human in mind, something soulful. I needed more faith to believe in a spontaneous Big Bang theory than to believe in a Creator of some kind, and I wasn't one for having much faith, so I decided to believe in God. I knew there had to be something beyond the flesh, something extraordinary outside my own understanding, an arbiter for the creation of the universe, a phenomenal Creator who began this menagerie of baby rabbits, Leica cameras, and Ryan Gosling.

Prude: Misconceptions of a Neo-Virgin

Stemming from a collection of scriptural references and stories I pieced together after eavesdropping on my parents' conversations and half-finished stories, I feared God's judgment. Left to my own devices, I complicated the gospel of love with His wrath and misaligned thoughts from the Old Testament. Theories that a giant, supernatural, white-bearded chap would strike me with a two by four—or a bolt of lightening if wood weren't available—should I wear a cotton and polyester blend, according to the Holy Code in Leviticus, were misconstrued imaginations from my little only-child brain, aged eight. My fear grew from there, and I became frightfully religious, minus a penchant for Queen, The Rolling Stones, and the TV show Cheers.

My parents never introduced me to the religious rules concerning virginity, never instilled the fear of God into my life. Far from it. They were a gentle couple, caring, articulate, highly intelligent, unconditionally loving, happy-go-lucky, the kind you secretly despise because everything is working out just tickety-boo. For being religious leaders themselves, they never forced their faith on me. They hadn't even christened me at birth. Discipline was only for my own safety, and discussions of sex were never followed by the word sinful. I surmised that it was a nice thing to do with your one and only, too exclusive to be shared with any other.

The general reasons I desired to maintain my virgin status came from an amalgamation of administering parental advice, waiting for a man who didn't place a girl's underwear on notice boards (more on this later), and of course, the fear of God Almighty. If I thought God might strike me with one billion volts of electricity should I trespass over the pre-marital sexual commandment, then I was quite content to say no before saying wedding vows.

When I reached the tween years, I attended an all-girls school. Its walls were constructed from Georgian stone with vast enough space to host hundreds of cute girls adorned in red berets and navy kilts. Our uniform was somewhat to be admired, along with the lyrics to our school anthem:

Within these walls of grey, how much do we gather?
Friendship and laughter gay! Gifts indeed.

It was a dated hymn, admittedly. Assembly started off our day with teachers gowned in black, sitting on stage, our Headteacher speaking in Latin. Think Hogwarts without the wands. There was a certain stature, a dignified decorum expected from the girls, so talk of boys was discussed through passed notes and bathroom banter. I would have thought my purity a perfect fit for this setting. But it was not 1925. Despite formal architecture, the values no longer matched, and my reluctance to lose my virginity was so well known that one boy from a neighboring school wanted to profile me in his school's gazette. A bit harsh, I thought, especially as they said they needed something to fill the sports section.

Still, I was unfazed. Did I share this reasoning with my friends? Absolutely not. No one understood God, and to be frank, neither did I. I appreciated sex's exclusivity, and it worked for my parents' loving marriage, filled with too much tickling and soppy affections for my liking, but it was preferable over raucous fighting and teary children. I was fifteen and going on what I experienced and what I knew. I was hardly going to go by the advice of people the same age who called me "boobless" when they thought I wasn't listening. They only wanted me to do it because they were doing it, and everybody wanted me in their gang, just only on their terms.

And, let's face it, if God, or what I called "the Essence," inspired thoughts of prophets to write incredibly accurate and fulfilled predictions of the events in the history of man, then perhaps I should take note of the advice given on how to live my life–and that included whether I should or should not sleep with some boy who was nicked-named "poop-head." Why that guy was called "poop-head," I had no idea; why God suggested we should save sex for marriage also was a mystery. In short, I simply trusted that the arbiter of the universe surely knew how we should look after ourselves.

By the time I entered high school, I was infamous with the boys at the neighboring school as one of the last remaining virgins in my year, which to them meant that I was one of the last remaining virgins on Planet Earth. It wasn't long until there was a photograph of me pinned to their school notice board, a picture my uncle had taken of me in Los Angeles.

"How nice." I blushed upon hearing of the photograph's new home. I wonder who put it up there? Am I next to their big crushes? Elle Macpherson? Linda Evangelista? Wait...how did they get the picture? I grew increasingly intrigued concerning the whereabouts of this snapshot and why, oh why, it was next to all the pictures of supermodels. I mean, I was pretty if you squinted your eyes and looked directly toward the sun, but I wasn't Christy Turlington.

I discovered that it wasn't a girl-crush picture by bribing my friend James with a can of Coke and a Kit Kat. Rather, its placement on the board had a different agenda: I was the target to see which boy could get me to lose my virginity. Bets were being thrown, and for the record, I wasn't situated next to the same beautiful models of George Michael's Freedom 90 music video. There were no supermodels. I, or more accurately, my photograph, was pinned next to a pair of Mrs. Stanton's laundered underwear, ones that had been stolen from her own chest of drawers when her daughter threw a secret house party.

This was how our schools rolled.

I suffered this ribbing continuously. I could expect such when my lifestyle didn't match that of The Full Monty or Pulp Fiction. I preferred singing along to Julie Andrews as she pranced about on that hilltop in The Sound of Music (she was clearly helicoptered in) more than watching Uma Thurman get stabbed in the chest with an intra-cardiac injection. But some people had an issue with my preferences. Of course, the words frigid and uptight were often put to good use, and phrases like "She's about as much fun as Margaret Thatcher" were spurted around in my home economics class. I had witty quips ready to contest such Marge jokes: "Maybe Margaret is a tiger in the bedroom. You don't know. And might I add, it wasn't her sex life that won us the Falklands war."

Still my stigma grew. Even the teachers got involved.

"Miss, I appear to have only got a D on my natural science paper?" I asked my Physics teacher.

"That's probably because you're a virgin." They were all in on it.

My face suddenly flushed to an unflattering lobster shade.

I missed the simpler days of being thirteen, when the only obsessions my girlfriends had were the newly invented Venus Lady Shave and learning how to arabesque on ice-skates. But a new season of self-sabotage had become the rage. Amphetamines, drinking cider 'til you could puke, and learning all the lyrics to Cypress Hill's Black Sunday album (can they construct a sentence without a swear word?)—these were the things to be doing with our spare time.

I had contemplated involving myself in some friends' recreational activities one night when one of them piped up with a revelatory idea: "Let's see how many ecstasy tablets we can take!"

A few of her friends excitedly clapped their hands, until I responded: "Until what? Death?"

I needed an outlet for my theory of purity to be understood, for my peers to see it my way. Theater was my canvas in order to express the real virginal me. I was no prude; I was not uptight; I could talk about sex like it was going out of fashion if necessary. Still, I wondered why we had to talk about it at all. Is it Oxygen? No. Did sex hang the moon? No, it did not. Can it tell a joke? Well, sometimes. The world needed to learn a fresh perspective, and my theatrical debut was the perfect place to be finally heard.

I invented plays: full-blown scripts with titles I trusted were subtle enough to hide that this was a self-portrayal of my life. I pitched these new titles to my drama group with the hope they'd take them on, make a huge production for both the boys' and girls' schools, and within their Stanislavski method acting, their revelatory rehearsals, they would all choose to abstain from sex. Then the pressure would be off, we'd invite chivalry back into the classroom with open arms, and they'd see the deeper meaning of the word relationship. I imagined that as they recited their lines, they would be mind-blown by the brilliance of holding out, and they'd make me the target, not of their sexual conquests, but of their gratitude. You know, something like, "Without Carrie Lloyd, we'd not have found purity so alluring; we would not have found Jesus Christ," or anything along those lines. Did I mention I loved drama?

Then one day during theater class, Mr. Clemeson spoke the words that had filled my daydreams for months.

"What shows are we thinking of doing for this year's production?"

He had opened the floor for suggestions! This was my chance. "I was thinking we should look at the more independent productions, less mainstream theatrical numbers. More art-house storylines?" I coughed up.

"Do you have anything in mind, Carrie?"

"Well, I was thinking perhaps the works of new writers, you know, explore a less trodden ground?"

"That's a nice idea. Anyone else like that option?"

A grumble of agreement came from a bunch of less enthused females.

"There are a few new scripts I've found…." I fingered through my papers as if the idea just sprang to mind.

"Okay. Why don't you share them with us?" Mr. Clemeson found a space to rest, looking up at the sky, ready to be inspired.

Melissa, sitting next to me, nearly choked me on her Fahrenheit perfume as she edged up to look over my shoulder.

"Well, there's one called The Lone Virgin."

Mr. Clemeson was instantly unimpressed.

"It's about a girl who develops supernatural powers, secretly, without the knowledge of her fellow schoolmates. Then Jesus Christ comes to save all the virgins, and everyone else is thrown into an active volcano. It's…a dark comedy."

"Uh-huh. Well, it's one to consider. Anyone else have any—"

"I do have another one that, I think, might be better than the first one. That one is called Bathed in the Blood of Virgins. It's about a planet where people never die because of the particular type of bathing materials they use."

Mr. Clemeson laughed. "That's actually quite funny. Is that a dark comedy too?"

"No. It's a hard-hitting drama. And it's not biographical. Not biographical at all."

"Did you write these yourself, Carrie?" Mr. Clemeson frowned.

The class turned around to see my reaction.

Silence.

I narrowed my eyes. "Who told you?"

The world wasn't ready for my talents to match that of the playwright, Noel Coward. Perhaps saving one's virginity would come back in fashion like the trend of the bell-bottom flare. One thing was certain: To be truly understood about sexuality was a lost cause. Coward had to hide his homosexuality, and I, another brilliant playwright in the making, had to hide my lack of sexual experience.

Some days it felt like it was just me and Margaret Thatcher against the world, having to brace myself on entering school to see who would throw the line: "Have you popped your cherry yet, Carrie?" I'd secretly note a beautiful boy and imagine us falling in love, but the reality was, no one felt the same way I did. No one wanted to save it for one person. They wanted to spread seedless nothings to a range of people to gain experience, to exert some super power, to defy their youth, to pretend they weren't fifteen, but twenty-five.

If I didn't comply, I wasn't worth spending much time on. Why would a guy want to spend a moment with a girl who wouldn't give anything other than witty quips and Arthur Miller recitals? This subtle prejudice toward my choices made me more determined to hold out. Prejudice always makes us want to revolt because it is never delivered from the stance of goodness, but rather the stance of someone else's fear. I wanted the sophisticated approach, the one where a strong dashing Adonis might come and save me from a burning building, ask me to marry him just after he's asked me what my name is. He'd whisk me down the ladder to safety, and we'd wed the next week in a small but dazzling ceremony. Then it's game on—but not before. I was pretty sure I'd seen the scars left on those who'd been struck by lightening, so before was simply not an option.

Within the teenage era, one thing I had begun to learn was that reasoning wasn't the "done thing." Popularity was all the rage. No matter how talented I was at debating a point, competition and the art of influence had a more profound effect on my happiness than being kind to myself. My real question was: What was the harm in waiting? Why was I being mocked for choosing to save sex? No one would laugh in the face of an investor who had spent ten years saving all his money to place it into a dream property. Was this not just all about goal setting and planning? Was I expected to blow my "money" on some immature guy whose only aim was to be the one who took my picture off the wall? Now that seemed like a bad investment, poor planning, and—oh look, we're back to mortgages again.

CHAPTER 3

Damned if You Do, Damned if You Don't

I n 1995, Britain was sending its forces to join the longest siege of a capital city in the history of modern warfare (Sarajevo), unemployment was on the rise, and the Queen Mother had a rather traumatic hip operation, but most importantly, Carrie Lloyd, age fifteen, still wouldn't "put out." To my schoolmates I had become a national tragedy. A bit like when Ross cheated on Rachel with that photocopier chick in *Friends*.

I had heard it was different for kids in America, but for the other teens and me in the UK, there was no middle ground. If a girl slept with too many men, she could expect much derogatory name-calling, comparing her to the likes of Polly Adler, one of New York's notorious madams in history. She wouldn't be eaten by dogs to the point of being unrecognizable like that infamous queen, Jezebel, in the Old Testament, but the insults would still be pretty rough. If she didn't sleep with anyone at all (that would have been me), then she would be compared to a brick wall. She had nothing to offer and gave off the idea that she probably read *The National Geographic* in her spare time or wore briefs with pictures of Snoopy on them. Only one of those statements was true in my case. To this day I have never read an issue of *National Geographic*.

Meanwhile for the boys, should one of them have found a fair maiden to sexually experiment on, he would have had a small ceremonial party thrown in his honor to celebrate his achievement, his passage into "adulthood." If his father were rich enough, he'd buy his son a bed made of pure mahogany on which to make real notches of his conquests. Sure, he might still be too young to drink, file a tax return, or even drive a car, but at least he could have uncomfortable coital with a girl he'd probably never be in touch with two weeks after the event, let alone two years. His peers, coaches, and others in modern society would offer him a round of applause, raising a toast of congratulations nonetheless.

The girls at my school were already up to their thighs in ferocious sexual warfare—over boys. Same-sex establishments weren't necessarily built from the same ilk as mixed-sex comprehensive schools. Boys were a delicacy to us, like a Godiva truffle: They weren't to be touched or looked upon, apart from certain times of the year, be it in rehearsals for our joint-school annual musical *West Side Story* or when we peered through the fence of the boys' sports field to watch them play Rugby every other weekend. To get around these austere restrictions, we invented school "projects" to include the male form.

"Let's be cheerleaders for the boys Rugby team!" Charlie suggested. Now she had an actual interest in the sport, but the rest of us were very happy to collate and design uniforms—attractive ones—to entice our prey, I mean, to support our fellow peers.

"Since when do Rugby teams have cheerleaders?" Scott, one of our guy friends from the neighboring school, asked. "We're not America for crying out loud. I should be able to have my ear ripped off or my cartilage dangling from my kneecap without twelve pathetic girls screaming at decibels none of us invited. Why don't you pluck your nails, or whatever it is you do, and leave us to get on with the sport?" He skulked off, insulted, possibly terrified by the idea of our brilliant, ultra feminine, blue glitter hoodies infiltrating such a masculine sport.

We stared at him as he walked off, entranced like the bunch of buffoons that we were.

"Isn't he dreamy?" Charlie sighed.

Skyline fences and rules of no late-night stone throwing at the boy's school dormitory windows aside, we all knew each other. The boys knew the girls, the girls knew the boys. There was Billy, Buddy, Scott, Maxy, Jack, Francis, 200 other boys whose names I forget, and Liam, who smelt of Fahrenheit cologne, so Melissa had bought her own bottle of the stuff.

"You smell like a middle-aged man," I retorted to her in our religious education class.

"I smell like Liam." She smiled, inhaling her jumper like she was some sort of glue-addict.

I had an interest in the lads like most teenage girls do, but the desire to save myself was still very strong. Uncomfortably, the boys all knew my stance on sex, that it was a vetoed option to me and that I had no plan to do it before marriage. I'd date each boy for about six weeks, which was about the time he realized I wouldn't have sex. Then he'd move on to one of my friends in the hope that she would meet his needs.

Charmed, I'm sure.

They also knew that I would not utter one swear word after catching me singing *The Birdie Song* (also known as the "Chicken Dance") at

Charlie's birthday party a few years before, prancing and flapping around like a big bird, shouting along to the lyrics while a small crowd stood watching me: *With a little bit of this and a little bit of that and shake your BEEP, don't be so rude!* Censoring the word *bum* for a synthesized electronic *beep* from my own vocals made sense to me. I turned to find a small crowd in astonishment.

"Did you just censor *The Birdie Song*, Carrie?" Charlie asked.

"I don't feel comfortable with these questions," I replied. Truth was, I secretly feared that I might regret such vocabulary on the Day of Judgment.

I did meet a boy named Jack who knew my boundaries but took a chance dating me anyway. All was well at Camp Virgin. We went on a lot of adventures, and because he looked very much like Damon Albarn from *Blur*, a heartthrob for me at the time, I lived in a small fantasyland, pretending to be Justine Frischmann, Damon Albarn's press-reported girlfriend. It helped that Jack played the guitar too.

One girl from my class, Collette, despised me. Loathed me. She was also friends with Jack and had dated his friend until recently. She was known to have had quite a bit of sex by sixteen, and because I had been doing the exact opposite, my lifestyle often made fighters out of my fellow females. Shame comes in seclusion and secrecy, but often shows itself in judgment against others. As her name became marred with another type of label, her shame manifested in defensiveness, the desire to lead everyone the same way, and by throwing judgment toward those who carried the opposite perspective. The attack was worse for me, since it eventually became obvious that I was dating the boy she really wanted.

Perhaps she thought he was Damon Albarn too. I had temptations to confess, "You know that's not really Damon Albarn. He's just a teenage boy who does questionable Al Pacino impressions within an awkward silence, one who can't stop eating Aniseed candy."

Collette phoned Jack most nights. These were heavy-handed conversations with one very clear purpose—to win. "Why are you dating her? She won't put out. She won't give you what you want. But I can. Man, you'd have way more fun with me."

Armageddon arrived at Classroom 13 one day, when I was quite frankly done with her incessant, spiteful backlash.

"I got an A in history! I've never had that before!" cried Ruby, a girl who had struggled with dyslexia since she was eleven. This was a triumph for her, and a group of us applauded, mounding into a human pile around her.

"Thank God you've achieved something this year because it's certainly not your ability to understand a concept called *style*," replied Collette snidely.

Ruby looked deflated, readjusted her glasses, and scuttled off to the bathroom.

After an entire two years of derogatory comments from Collette toward anyone with a victory, my justice-driven heart piped up. "Oh will you just shut up!" I declared.

If looks could kill, then she had just shot me in the head fifteen times. Trembling, anxious, I pretended to look away as I gnawed on a piece of chocolate gateaux that was going around the class, a celebration for the end of the semester.

"You know, I've been meaning to say this for a while, Carrie, but no man will ever fall in love with you. Your boyfriend clearly fancies me. I know because we were on the phone last night talking for hours."

I responded blithely, "Your phone bill must have cost a fortune."

Walking closer to me, she piqued her head up in the air and narrowed her eyes. She believed her sexual experience was her winning factor, and she was armed to launch an attack.

The rest of the girls watched wide-eyed at the bloodshed about to ensue.

"You're afraid. Too freaky for Jesus, too frigid for any man to stay with you," she went on. "He'd get more entertainment from arranging matches than listening to you talk. I mean, what do you do every evening? I bet you're a pro at Trivial Pursuit. He'll dump you in a week in search for a real woman. Just like the rest of them. Mark my words."

The other girls gasped in horror at the lowness of the blow. I took a look at her, spied the gateaux, surveyed the area I was standing in, and took another squinted glance at her.

"You think I can't score?" I asked. Then I lifted my hand and pitched the cake right between her eyes. My aim perfectly hit the bridge of her nose, and the cream clung for dear life in her hair.

"I think I scored that time." I smiled, stunned that I had successfully thrown an object forward for a change.

Collette stormed out.

The small crowd watched Collette leave then turned to me with a huge round of applause.

I was tempted to take a bow, but I didn't want to push the boundaries of the compassion I had just won. I congratulated myself for weeks after that, believing that I had finally conquered Colette and her conniving jealousy. However, despite my seemingly strong stance against her that day, I couldn't help but take her comments to heart. I was searching to understand myself. We all were. In this conflict, I wondered if being popular had taken too much governance in my life. I didn't become arrogant; I became people pleasing. My drug of choice in my teens was other people's affections. Was I beautiful? Did my morality matter? Was there truth in Colette's comments? Would men be uninterested in me because I would not give them what they coveted most? Would I find a man who could look past his own needs to honor mine? How could I ignore Colette's words when I surveyed the expectations of my generation's sexual promiscuity?

For one gender, sexual freedom meant being donned with a scarlet letter; for the other, a stuffed and mounted trophy that friends often referred to in admiration. The desire for freedom from religious and societal restriction in the 1920s, mixed with the disillusionment brought by war, gradually and radically shifted the supply and demand for sex. By the late sixties, it was "free love;" *free* in this case meaning, free from responsibility and commitment. Now one could sleep with any number of people. The more we accepted that sex didn't need to be based in love, the more we began to focus on our needs rather than someone else's. Contraception was obviously a necessity, the freedom and the right to choose when we want to get pregnant useful, but the packet never came with an emotional health disclaimer warning us to be responsible with our hearts, our brains and its neurons. Most talk about the sixties as being the most liberal era and revolutionary in freedom, but I have a different point of view: Women ended up becoming more entrapped, fighting with competition and comparison, and utilizing various manipulative attempts hoping to catch the eye of a hunter.

Perhaps a decade before the invention of the contraceptive pill it was more socially acceptable, even expected, for men to fight for a girl. They had to seriously consider their intentions, showing commitment for marriage prior to sleeping with her. Pre-1967 men had to take responsibility, and if they were known to bed an "honest" woman, they were ostracized by friends for treating her dishonorably, for putting her at risk of unwed pregnancy. However, thanks to a new generation that believed sexuality was repressed, a revolt occurred. The free-love society changed the male attitude—and women's. People could pick and choose a temporary mate, learning not to take the responsibility for each other's hearts quite so seriously. The contraceptive pill was a great invention, but like all freedom, we learned how to misuse it.

Meanwhile, women were fighting for someone, anyone to love them. The curse of Eve, as I like to call it, formed this idea from the very beginning of creation that women were created to be the helper, or the *ezer kenegdo* to Adam. It wasn't that the original intention of being a helpmate was evil, but that it was misinterpreted through the curse. The curse says, "Everything will be redeemed once I have found my husband. Once I'm with him, I will be happier and have found my purpose. I was made for him and nothing else. I was formed to procreate for the human race."

So, until then, until the man of her dreams has materialized with some diamond attached that shines brighter than Galadriel from *Lord of the Rings,* she'll flick through *InStyle* until her fingers bleed, making mood boards based on what eye color she thinks her future husband will have. *Without him, we are nothing*, or so society could make us feel. Guests at dinner parties would forever feel a bizarre responsibility to fix up single ladies with *someone*. Surely it is not okay for a woman—especially in the Church—to be single in her thirties and beyond.

Because we believed the idea that we were worthless, helpless without a man, it became about survival of the fittest *within the same sex.* So with all our sexual freedom and modern society's double standard of *stag* labels for men and derogatory labels for women, our culture created, even celebrated, a genre of females who had become more competitive with each other. After all, even in pre-selfie eras, women were always designed to nest and look out for threats. The feminist movement hadn't helped us, nor had the Spice Girls invention of "girl power" encouraged us to be *for* each other when it came to acquiring a man. The tilting of the hips, the playing with the hair in conversation with another person's man, the over-enthusiastic laughing at his less-than-best jokes were just small indicators of an increasing problem. Placing the heartbreak, the emotional vulnerability that exceeded intimacy, the biblical precepts, and the rise in statistics of Chlamydia aside, *this* was another major issue about sex that caused me concern. Back then, no one else seemed to mention it, and still to this day, few are aware of its toxicity.

Ten years after I tossed cake at Colette's face, I ran into another fellow schoolmate, Coco, who had been in the room on that infamous day. What I didn't know until our reunion in the pub was that she had followed Collette into the corridor after the incident. Coco and I barely knew each other; we weren't bosom buddies or anything even close to it. Yet in the hallway of our school Coco had begun to fight for my right to choose, for the freedom to hold myself ready for the right guy. Despite my firm opinion that sisterhood was well and truly buried, it appeared it had in fact been resurrected, or at least had woken up from a coma.

As she and Collette argued, another teacher intervened, asking what the problem was.

"Collette is being cruel to Carrie about her choice to keep her v-plates."

"Oh well, carry on then," the teacher responded. "I'll have to give you a detention obviously for causing a racket in the hallway, but I think it's time Collette heard everyone's heart on the matter."

Coco puffed herself up, knowing that Collette had quite the mean streak, and began her speech: "Just because you made a decision to flounce about with sixteen-year-old boys doesn't mean your shame has to become someone else's nightmare. Your self-loathing character can go and jump off a precipice, because quite frankly, you're bringing the entire class down. I'm sick to death of seeing happy girls with less chocolate in their hair being pummeled down with your verbal bullying. You want her boyfriend? Go get him, but he'll never be enough for you. No one ever will. You sold all your shares months ago when you slept with what's-his-face. Destroying a girl who doesn't need to show boys her private parts in order to find herself is as helpful for female empowerment as a ham sandwich."

Coco straightened herself out, checking to see that the teacher was still there in fear of grievous bodily harm about to take place. She was safe, noting Mrs. Stanton's raised eyebrows, her face stoic to keep from smiling. Some sisters do appreciate it when we fight for each other. Imagine this being the Women's Suffrage movement with women chaining themselves to the gates of the House of Commons in Westminster or picketing outside the White House, fighting for the right to vote. Only on this occasion, it involved cake batter and a little too much of an over-share.

For pride's sake, Collette remained stone-faced, clearly wishing to retaliate, but Coco's argument stumped her.

"Mrs. Stanton, let me know when that detention is. I will gladly serve for what, I believe, was totally worth it." Coco smoothed out her uniform, smiled, and walked away, knees knocking, yet triumphant.

You see, there were some girls in my school who felt it only fair for a girl to have a choice, for a girl to have her own path. And any argument that suggested I should have sex before I was ready only came from a place of fear, people pleasing, or a strange camaraderie push of conglomerate sexual experimentation. None of it was from a place of kindness. No one was in love with anyone; we were too young to know the meaning of real love. Whilst my school peers might have dished out labels, I was searching for authenticity, for protection in such vulnerability, like the kind of love and security my parents had with each other.

Disappointingly, competition between women didn't cease when I graduated school. In fact, it only grew worse, and it continued to baffle me beyond university and even into the workplace. I remember being friends with a bunch of women who worked for MTV in the height of its popularity. By the time I began my first job, female creatives had become more established in the very much male dominated, chauvinistic world of advertising. Such clever banter between the sexes always left me enjoying their company, even delighted to be a female. But when I began to date one of their colleagues at MTV, it seemed as if overnight the women were texting him for "girlfriend-free time," deliberately asking him not to bring me along. When passing them on the street, I'd wave, but they'd cross over, pretending not to see me. Others would ramp up the flirtatiousness and upgrade their relationship level from being "a good friend of his" to now being "his best friend."

Female competition was as potent as it was in grade school, only now the tricks were more lucid, more manipulative, and harder to catch with a naked eye. If their warnings of my sexual abstinence weren't enough to detract my boyfriend from still coming my way, then they'd employ seductive flirtations and provocative messages. This activity was always carried out in secret, loud enough for me to notice but quiet enough for me to be unable to say something without seeming jealous.

A few of these girls were not just colleagues but friends I'd known for a long while. One in particular took it upon herself to spread her opinion about how "weird" she felt our relationship was now that we had moved from friends to dating exclusively. At the same time she would message him on Facebook, telling him to check out inappropriate pictures of her and her girlfriends' attempts at pole dancing in a nightclub—all in private messages, of course.

It would be at this point where the men either knew how to have strong boundaries around these types of "sisters," stating clearly where our relationship was at, or they didn't know how to say *no*, and I would be faced with more warfare, more misunderstanding, more confusion. By my late twenties I was turning up to pubs equipped for battle with thermal imaging lenses ready to scan through the soul of the next woman who wanted to create her war with me. Okay, that bit isn't true, but I came close a few times. It can be a little barbaric out there these days.

It took discernment, powerful men with decent boundaries, and exiting the media industry for me to see that the healthiest of women, the ones who believed in themselves, didn't have time for antics. Unfortunately, I found that the Church wasn't immune. In that covenant-focused community, the pressure to wed intensified the female desire to be with and find fulfillment in a man. Between the 1:4, male/female ratio (in most cases) and the over-analytical approach to how men communicated with us women, the Christian dating world was just embarrassing. Men became overly cautious to text a girl for coffee in case she would, in response, see it as the "first step" to a marriage proposal. And the girls? Some were just as competitive, just as threatened by other attractive women.

Healthy women, whether inside the Church or out, dispelled the belief that there was only one single man available to twenty single women. They trusted in God's timing over their own wedding plans, and they found any occasion to celebrate another woman's victories. It took a decade, and I had to learn what to look for.

Cut to a moment about a year ago, when I witnessed something that clinched the beauty of what female empowerment can really look like. I was taking part in a guest panel for TBN UK's talk show, *The London Sessions with Cynthia Garrett*. As I do with all media and press, I braced myself for the worst, deciding beforehand to treat everyone the way I'd like to be treated—with encouragement, with a powerful self-security that isn't intimidated by another's greatness. For women in the entertainment industry, the threat of other women can be very real. Women are taught to size each other up and make comparisons—*is she younger, thinner, prettier?*

Damned if You Do, Damned if You Don't

What is she trying to do here, replace me? An hour in, however, and the only weapon used on me was a metal case of MAC cosmetics. The make-up artists in the room and the two of us women contributing to the show were laughing so much my mascara had to be redone.

I walked on set and saw Cynthia—stunning, beautiful, and vivacious in character as well as style. Her previous rock-and-roll lifestyle, along with her brother, Lenny Kravitz, being one of the most prolific rock stars of the twenty-first century, could pose as an instant threat to anyone who may not know her. But it didn't take more than a few minutes for me to turn to her while they were testing sound on stage and go straight for the jugular: "I bet women around you in your past didn't know what to do with you, did they?"

"I was about ask the same about you," she laughed. We both winked at each other, an exchange of acceptance in the circle of female trust and understanding.

"I found the right women to have around me," she explained. "Women who chose to understand instead of compete. Women who were not intimidated by someone else's character because they knew the power of their own." She was full of class, dignified with a sense of self that I was attracted to. It left me at ease, never having to hide my own self, my own worth. Powerful women welcome other powerful women around them.

As we began to record in the studio, Cynthia knew all of us women on the panel were rooting for her. Her nerves dispersed, her voice strengthened, our smiles disengaged any pre-show tension, and the spirit of encouragement shifted the entire studio. We began to tap into wisdom that surprised us.

High from the show's atmosphere, I was weak at the knees, this time for excitement's sake, to see women reach out to the hearts of the audience, to the women who came to learn more about healthier views of beauty and sex. I sat down next to Cynthia in the green room after we were done, both of us grateful for our work. The men who led the network surrounded us, free to be the kings they wanted to be, nurtured by us. No aggressive feminist movement was about to erupt because even that would be denying who we really were—women who had different voices, women who weren't trying to be men nor trying to win men, just women who wanted to do good within a sense of unity.

The need to have it all, be it all, win it all, to fight to our last breath hasn't always been around. Competition with other women defines so much of who we are meant to be these days that instead of finding out who we really are, we end up living lives as carbon copies of each other. Somewhere down the procreation route, women thought they'd win the game by sleeping with men. Sisters couldn't fight for or bring up a standard anymore; they couldn't encourage each other to be fought for, to say *no* to the "any takers."

If Collette or the MTV girls had been for rather than against me, would I have ever begun to question my own principles? Or would I have learned the importance of female encouragement instead? Would I have questioned why I felt it was important not to give everything away to a man who wanted it?

Women were always meant to be *for* each other, never against. If we were against each other, it was only because we were inherently against ourselves. I have never seen competition be exercised in women who really love themselves. Women who know their identities never play territorial warfare concerning men. They have enough self-love, enough self-belief not to seek validation beyond their own souls. Perhaps it takes time to discover the truth of who we are. Perhaps it's maturity that finally ends the need to override another female's existence, but there are women who, even in their later years, still vie for the love of married men, who still give themselves away in order to gain a little attention.

This battle could be over if we discovered how powerful we could be *together*. To cut our reason for existing into just two purposes, being "Eve the helper" to a man and "bun warmer" for the babies, limits our potential. We give ourselves the one option of being emotionally dependent on our romantic relationships and then suffer a psychological breakdown when Adam wants to call it a day. Is this really what we want to pass on to the next generation of women?

Sitting with Cynthia and the other guests on the show, we shared stories of our own lives, finding each other fascinating in our journeys. To my right was a piece of chocolate cake, not dissimilar to the gateaux I'd thrown at Collette twenty years before. I surveyed the land of my new favorite women, all fighting for righteousness, for female identity, for a "daughtership" approach to God, one where there was enough love (and enough dessert) to go around. We were women with four forks and one piece of chocolate cake, enjoying it the way it was meant to be enjoyed— together, fight-free.

CHAPTER 4

Coping or Copping Out?

4:00 a.m. I'm seventeen. Lying face down on the ground in the boy's school playing field, spread out like a starfish. Like you do. Flashlights were flickering in the distance and around the playing field, possibly school security, possibly police. My friend Skye had managed to find a tree the width of a rolling pin to hide behind; others scattered amidst the cars. I had nothing, so I flung myself to the ground, hoping the grass would swallow me up. Jumping over the gates of the boys' school swimming pool had become our usual tradition after clubbing on Saturday nights. I was soaked through from the open-air pool since, as was always the case, I hadn't brought a towel.

Trespassing and taking a casual dip in the chlorine pond was forbidden, probably illegal, but I was young, reckless, and still somehow managing to stay reasonably safe. I didn't take ecstasy or speed. I didn't have sex. Thanks to my emetophobia (my irrational fear of throwing up), I didn't drink, too scared that it might make me sick. But I refused to be a total outcast from civilization, so this little activity was one of the only rebellious ways to feel included, like I belonged.

"You'd make a terrible marine," Skye whispered, as she peered around the two-inch girthed tree, watching me eight feet away, spread-eagled, soaked, confused.

Others had also discovered our interest in jumping the pool gates, but unfortunately for them, they were completely unaware that they were about to be caught due to the amount of acid they were tripping on, quite literally.

"Oh, look—it's all springy!" I could hear one of them shout and splash. "I think it's elastic enough for me to walk on the water. Let me try."

You'll need Jesus for that, Love, not a square of hallucinogens, I thought.

As the searchlights crept closer, Skye noted it was indeed the police. "We have about five seconds to leg it to the bridge over there, or we can just stay here and get arrested? Which one? Your legs decide."

Neither of us liked the latter option. Running it was.

We escaped, victorious. To this day I have no clue on the fate of those left at the pool pushing the water up and down as if it were a bouncy castle, but I was free—from the police at least. As much as we all laughed, it had been one of many close calls, and I didn't like thinking about how serious it could have become if we had been arrested. I wanted rapport, I wanted to belong to a group of accepting friends, but often it was at the cost of my own values and true nature. Deep down, I actually valued being honest, respecting authority, trusting that rules existed for our benefit. If I were being my authentic self, I wouldn't have played so close to the edge. A game of Boggle would have sufficed.

At seventeen, this was my life. My desperate attempts to connect to my peers, or at least not be rejected by them, was clashing with my inner desire to be kind and honorable, to listen to my parents, to be understood, and to make sure God wasn't angry with me. The task of being a chameleon to all those for whom I cared was getting a little out of hand. There were others in my school who were not having sex, like myself, but they were the leading intellects. They studied root words of dead languages, enjoyed conversations about political positions, inhaled books written by philosophers in one breath, exhaled the words of Aristotle with the next. Every class needed a geek or two, so these weren't expected to sleep around or run half-naked through the grass from the police in the middle of the night. I wasn't completely lacking in the brain department, but I was known for cleverness and humor more than an impressive vocabulary, my stage acting and dance moves more than my debate skills.

I attempted to find my people, my tribe. Like most teens, if I had to be labeled at all, then I preferred being "cool." The other options weren't quite to my liking and certainly didn't make life easier. I searched for the more socially acceptable cliques, of which there were a few, but when it came down to it, I didn't quite feel like Carrie with them. I wasn't interested in Ouija board games in the attic of the school and had nothing to offer when other girls talked about their sexual exploits.

I had to spread myself thinly, fitting in with everyone generally but not too many people specifically. I was grateful for those friends who were similar to me and not so bogged down by catty warfare. Perhaps it was that desire for a certain level of anonymity that drew us together, made us ready for the latest phenomenon that was taking over the world: rave festivals and super clubs. Cream in Liverpool, The Hacienda in Manchester, Ministry of Sound in London, and Bungalow 8 in New York were the new weekend hot spots in the mid-nineties, and road tripping to raves the new pastime. Thousands would find themselves at pop-up dance parties in huge warehouses or rented stately homes in the country without too much notice ahead of time. Spontaneity was everything. So was being high. Really high. My aim was only to dance and then eat toast once home. Still, being around those taking narcotics was less lonely than being at someone's house where boyfriends and girlfriends would part ways into different bedrooms, leaving me behind to listen to BBC news in the living room.

As long as I was dispersed across a few different groups, I would never have to be constantly questioned, nor made to feel different from the rest for the things I *wouldn't* do. I was with people long enough to have a good time, but short enough to exit without much notice when found in a tight spot. Such tactics worked for about a year.

Until I fell in love.

Barney was utterly gorgeous. Dark hair, blue eyes, and a perfect smile, which was displayed often since he loved to laugh and actively sought things to joke about. He'd been with his former girlfriend, Sarah, for a while, but by the time I came onto the club scene, they'd been broken up for a bit. He was nineteen; I was seventeen. Only a two-year age gap, but in a couple of ways I felt like a twelve-year-old with Barney: 1) Sarah, his ex, owned a car (a bitter blow as I was still being chauffeured around by my mother); and 2) She and Barney had been intimate—and I don't mean a sharing of journal entries.

Nevertheless, Barney and I swiftly began dating. He bought me little presents. He picked me up in his car. Under my bed sat a box of treasures that Barney had given me: a stuffed lion that purred, music that we played in the car, cinema stubs, his jumper doused in Tommy Hilfiger cologne, a picture of *that smile* in a locket I sometimes wore around my neck. I was hooked and, as far as I was concerned, in love.

He understood all the implications of me being a virgin, and he never once pressured or expected me to go beyond my comfort level. He was gentle and had a tender heart. He longed for sexual connection, but he did what his mother taught him to do: to respect and treasure a woman, no matter what. I learned that most men appreciated a good personality, a hint of intelligence in a woman. They too wanted rapport, and although most wanted to find it through sex, Barney was open to discovering it through different ways with me. In order to let him know I was of *some* fun, and in the hope that he could connect to me as much as he might have done in a sexual relationship, I became a great flirt with jovial banter, often replaying the latest in stand-up from our favorite comedians.

At the same time I was taking my first step into the world of romantic attachment, my other girlfriends were becoming fully sexually active. Still, I felt part of the gang now that I had a boyfriend, and although I hadn't gone "all the way," they were more than happy to note the effect love was having on their friend. I began wearing outfits that would make the most lenient of parents blush, changing at friends' houses to avoid alarming my parents. I was sharing a bed with a boy for the first time too, and even though I didn't do anything overtly sexual, it would be the first time I ever hid anything from my father. I started managing secrets and risks, thinking that I wasn't doing anything wrong.

Meanwhile Sarah, Barney's ex, would still visit his house to see his mum. On one occasion Sarah spontaneously ran upstairs to his room, saw a photograph of me on his wall, and ripped it down, screaming bloody murder. To put it lightly, she had not taken the breakup well. She took the information about Barney's new relationship even worse. The unfortunate thing was, thanks to my picture, she now knew what I looked like. She had a face to compare herself to, someone to hate, to *defeat*.

So she'd just happen to arrive at the same club we were at, always dolled up to the nines. In response, my outfits got shorter, tighter; my fake lashes got longer (at one point they could have provided shelter for three fully-grown adults).

While I might have been learning to drive to make up for my lack of non-mum transportation, Sarah still had something over me that intensified my despair as the weeks went on: There was a physical connection between her and Barney that I knew I couldn't beat with witty charm or flirtation. How much more did I need to do to compete with the intimacy they shared? Could I compete with it at all? Perhaps my skirt needed to be a little shorter? I crossed over more of my boundaries—a little more skin, a few more sexual references to make out I was in the know— but I couldn't bring myself to try things that would be labeled as "sexual activity." In some moments of my day, all the covering up, the pretense, the false vernacular of being something I didn't really care for was becoming exhausting…but prevail I did.

Although I was a believer in God and thought I understood that sex was to be treasured for marriage, I didn't have a clear motivation as to the *why*. Why should I save myself? I just did, and obeying it had so far kept me out of trouble. Dad had told me how special sex was, how awesome it was within a committed relationship, one in which you knew there was no change of mind. And why should I doubt my father about such things? He was the man who introduced me to the world, to the male form in general. He was the one who fought for me, provided for me, made me feel safe, took me on dates every Sunday, and valued me more than I valued myself. Why would I question anything he said? No one questions anything when the clear intention is love, and his certainly was.

Still, all of this was helpful information for guarding myself against men who were idiots, but Barney wasn't a jerk. He had a good heart, a genuine intention to know me. The black-and-white lines were fading, and the desire to connect more deeply only grew stronger. My God-given desire for intimacy was being influenced by the expectations of my culture, the late night, fun-filled partying, the dopamine-fuelled risk of seeking the unknown.

I'd come back on a Sunday after a weekend of clubbing, and my parents, enthusiastic about all my endeavors, would always be excited to hear my stories: "So what did you do? How is Barney? Has he been treating you well? Did you encourage him? Did you make sure you were complimentary? Was he complimentary to you? As long as my girl feels safe, as long as she is honored, I fear nothing," Pops would share, flicking *The Daily Telegraph* newspaper so that the corner would bend, displaying his right eye.

I'd look up somewhat regrettably from my soup to catch his face.

He'd smile and wink. "We're very proud of our daughter, aren't we, May?"

Mum would smile with a bashful tilt of the head and giggle at her husband's sweet adoration for her daughter.

I'd roll my eyes, embarrassed at all this love in their air. The truth was, such love made me uncomfortable; it always does when you've been lying. When we weren't travelling to massive fields to hear famous DJs with speakers the size of a multi-story car park, Barney's and my regular hangout was Central nightclub. The more fun we had, the more drugs some friends sought as their need to get a higher hit increased. We had all sorts of colorful people gracing our lives in those days. Our friend, Pete, in particular. I didn't know his last name; I don't think any of us did. The guy practically defined "life of the party." He was on everyone's speed dial for that necessary, bubbling personality. His vibrancy inspired us to play hard, laugh hard, ridding any dignity at the door. We were no longer there to impress; we were there to have a good time, and no party ended without him creating some grand exit. On one too many occasions Pete was found unconscious, and someone would drag him home to rest.

Constantly around this kind of crowd, it was a wonder my parents weren't worried: "I'd have a chat with you about the current pill-popping culture you're probably surrounded by, Carrie, but considering your vomit phobia thing, I doubt I need to?" They shared this with me whilst I snuggled into bed between them. They were watching their regular rendition of *Cheers*, and I was tucking into a bowl of Bran Flakes.

I stopped chomping and looked at him. "I'm wearing flannel pajamas, sitting between my parents, eating cereal, and watching Ted Danson. I think you're good for the drug talk, Pops."

"That's my girl."

At the same time, everything around me slowly started to feel strange, unfamiliar, unnerving. Nothing was wrong, but something wasn't quite right either. Take, for instance, my friends. Melissa started dating a bouncer at Central named Snitch, and from a few of her stories I deduced that he wasn't exactly a gentleman. I was accompanying other clubbing friends to clinics regularly for STD tests and morning-after pills, and when they puked up the pills due to their strength, along with Cocaine or MDMA, I promised myself I'd never get to that place. Even though I hadn't taken part in the act of sex or gone through the pain they experienced, at least I was providing them comfort and myself the intimate knowledge of what was really going on.

Then one day the phone rang with Barney asking if he could meet up. His tone didn't feel right, and so I didn't feel right. He drove me to a country lane nearby and then turned off the engine.

"We can't go out anymore," he said without looking at me.

I was speechless. I moved to hold his hand, but he pulled away. "But... but what did I do?"

"You didn't do anything. I think you're great and gorgeous and funny, and I've had the best time with you, but…I can't do this."

It made no sense. We never fought; we were always laughing. I was weeks away from taking my driving test. One out of two rectifications compared to Sarah was better than none. What more could he want? He cried as I laid my head back against the car seat, stunned. He just…he just *couldn't*.

I didn't eat for three days. I'd wake up in the night, wondering if he had changed his mind. My friends had the same hope, trusting that Barney was just having a bad week. By the weekend, soulless and a few pounds down in weight, Melissa and Skye decided to cheer me up by buying me an "Operation Get Barney Back" outfit. After spending more than two hours playing Paul Oakenfold music and adorning myself in a dress that made me feel like a million bucks, I walked to the club with my friends. Then I saw Barney. My stomach tied in knots.

"He can't take his eyes off you," Melissa responded.

"I think the outfit is working," I breathed.

"He's going to come back, babe. I can feel it."

I had hope. Great hope. This was all I wanted right? To be coveted by the man I coveted? It was a conquest, a destination. What other destination was there? My job at Virgin Megastore was enjoyable, but it was hardly a calling. But Barney—couldn't *Barney* be my calling? This was just a spat, a digressive phase. I felt a sense of relief again, rationalizing that perhaps not all was as lost as it seemed. In the closing hour, I walked out with his friend Matt. He too believed Barney was questioning if he had made the right decision. We waited for people to leave the club, and in the midst of the crowd, I saw Sarah sitting on some steps a block down, crying. Then I saw Barney, comforting her.

"But you're way hotter than Sarah!" shouted Melissa, as she joined Matt and I outside.

"It's not always about the hotness," I replied flatly. "Right, Matt?"

Matt was silent, trying to divert my attention by noting that he had been wearing black socks over his shoes the entire evening. It was a standard tactic to get into the club at night without having to go home and change trainers since having proper shoes was a must at clubs.

But I couldn't stop watching.

Barney saw me look at them together. He looked to the sky, back to me, and bowed his head.

Sarah began to walk in the other direction.

For a moment I looked to him with a questioning brow, wondering if he was going to walk toward me.

He got up from the steps he was sitting on with Sarah, took one step forward, then turned on his heel, and walked away into the dark, following her. Within a week her car was in his driveway and my photograph in the trashcan.

My mother reliantly came back to being the designated driver, my father the shoulder to cry on.

"He was so handsome," I said.

My dad kissed my forehead, letting me cry into him. "But a greater man will see who you really are and will never want to let go. Not my girl. Not you."

I couldn't see what he saw, but took note of it somewhere in my mind. Dad's love for me, his constant availability, made me feel all the worse for lying to him about my recent hedonistic conduct. I chose the quiet of the nights to cry as much as I could, hoping his playing of the Beatles would drown out my sadness.

Back at school I was glad for the distraction of homework and books. Friends tried to cheer me up, while I tried not to think of Sarah and Barney naked in bed together, making up for the months they had spent apart.

Coping or Copping Out?

One day a rumor spread quickly about a student from the boys'
school. No one knew exactly what happened or exactly whom it concerned.
Within an hour, the entire school had been rounded up to attend an
assembly in the great hall. Our Headteacher's voice echoed throughout the
abyss of the dated walls. Her aristocratic accent was almost identical to the
queen. She came across as austere, formal, and strict, with spectacles so
big we wondered if they were those comedy glasses one might pick up in a
fancy dress shop.

"It is with great sadness that I have to share with you the news of a
fellow student from the boys sixth form named Pete Riddle. He was found
early this morning in the school playing field. I do not think it would
be appropriate to say any more at this time. Just that our prayers and
condolences go to his mother, siblings, and friends."

Sixth form was my age—merely seventeen. The great hall was quiet.
Girls began to break down in tears. So the rumors were about Pete. Fun
Pete, crazy Pete, life-of-the-party Pete had been found hanging from a tree,
the same one Skye had hidden behind only months before. The come down
from the three wraps of speed he had taken the previous night had been
too much for him to bear, his own belt the weapon of choice.

As stories unfolded, we heard he had planned this for a while. Had
we known, could we, would we have done anything different? These were
the questions we thought without voicing. I thought of his mum and how
young he was and how naive we all were. We were just a crowd who knew
no surnames, who knew nothing about each other.

I looked to Melissa, also in shock. She was closer to Pete in friendship
than I was. She had a black eye.

Melissa caught me staring at her bruise and quickly lowered her eyes.
"Snitch didn't want me going out the way I looked. For the first time I held
my own ground, but instead, he ensured I hit the ground with my own face

as he pushed me out of his moving car."

Skye and I were horrified as she wept in front of us. I couldn't tell if she was crying for Pete or for the abusive relationship in which she now found herself.

For all our attempts to find joy in our youth, the light in our wonder years, our identities in the risk-taking, I questioned who the hell we thought we were. Our current lifestyle—the late night rides with strangers, all the "one more wrap for the road" claims, the lengths to be everything we thought we should be, miles away from who we really were—wasn't exactly productive. And in my own heartbreak over a relationship with a boy who could barely look at me in the same room the past few weeks, a boy for whom I'd compromised by lying about to my parents, I realized the connection I so longed for had never come.

For all the fun times, I never really knew Pete. As it turned out, I never really knew Barney either. My compensation to be known by Barney had brought me back to asking would a man ever truly know me, would any of them stay if I didn't place my body on the chopping board before marriage?

With a head full of fear and doubt, I found myself back at a place I hadn't been for a while, before the raves, before Pete's suicide, before the pain began. Folksworth Church always left a giant key under the mat for visitors. I biked up, walked inside, and sat alone in the pew.

Cold. Silent.

I was peaceful for the first time in months—a comforting yet haunting thought. With no one in the church, I tried to talk out loud. With nothing to lose, I yearned for wisdom greater than the voice of another seventeen year old. But nothing could pass my lips.

My life was most open to a sense of something greater when I was at my most vulnerable. Not too long before I couldn't hear His voice, I didn't have a relationship with God as such. With my ideas of "having it altogether" dismantled, I was, like many who encounter great loss, now looking for something beyond myself, beyond my control. And so, with a heavy but willing heart, I waited.

Then I heard it, that whisper so often and easily ignored.

"My little one." It wasn't an audible voice. It wasn't a voice within either. I instinctively knew it was *Him*. I know for those who don't believe in God, these conversations are nothing but an imagined chat with Tinker Bell or Santa Claus, yet whenever I am in doubt, my brain, my heart has nothing. And that's where something beyond myself always shows up, not in my knowing, but rather in my *unknowing*.

So there I was, alone in the church, poised like the barrel of a gun to start the race. I said out loud, "I'm here," careless about who might have been listening.

"What were you hoping to find in your journey?"

"Friendship. Understanding. Life. A way of coping," I replied with a question in my tone.

"Did you find it?"

"No. I was searching for some light, but I found more darkness. It's as if I'm stumbling for the switch, and while I'm trying to turn it on, I'm bumping into all these other people who are trying to do the same. We see glimpses of light in each other, but it doesn't last for long. The laughs turn into tears, emotional connection turns into physical expectations, courageous acts turn into tragedy, promises become broken, and treasures under my bed turn into tomorrow's trash."

I'd been told God's aim was to give us "abundant life," yet in my attempts to do what He suggested, I was more comfortless. I fit in exactly nowhere with no one. "I tried to do what You advised us to do, but I became more lonely," I said.

Then there was His question: "And in your attempts to fit in, do you feel more befriended now?"

I cried into my hands. I obviously didn't feel any less lonely than when I chose to stay on a lamp-lit path. The more I compromised myself, the further from God I was, the darker my path became. I wanted true freedom, but I kept grasping at it in the dark, stumbling for the switch.

Despite how hard the truth was to face, this was the kindest voice I had heard in a while. I felt known, I felt cared for. Just how much had the drug dealers considered Pete? How much were men caring for the women they were throwing out of moving cars? How fulfilled were we at the end of a night if none of us were truly able to see the results of our decisions, if none of us even knew each other's names?

I thought of my friend who recently had an abortion after not taking the contraceptive pill regularly. She kept the entire procedure a secret, went alone to the hospital without any real idea of what she was about to experience. Then, months later in a drunken state, she finally uttered her pain of passing blood into the toilet straight after she had administered the first procedure of the two-step abortion process. As she passed the blood, something started to slip and her instinctive nature was to catch it: the flesh and mass of a twelve-week-old fetus in her hand. She educated us to a horror that none of us knew. This wasn't on the national curriculum at school. These were the photos the National Health Service didn't want printed on the handouts. All of us felt terrible for not even knowing about her experience. Her shame rendered her mute, her unplanned grief made her trustless, while the abandonment from her boyfriend left her hopeless.

I lay down on the stone floor of the church, staying there for some time. He continued to talk to me while He still had me, which was understandable—He wasn't sure how long I was going to stay around to listen. I looked up to the ceiling, observing the Fibonacci arrangement of the pipes of the organ. The silence of the church, the magnificence of the organ and all it wasn't playing caught my attention. Like notes on a piano, all the keys are there to be played at some point, just not all at the same time. Perhaps the urges I found within myself God had planted in me for the right reasons at the right times—the desire for sex, the longing for excitement, for risk-taking included?

"In time, my little one, you will see when your fingers must miss certain notes. You're learning already. This wisdom can only come from me. "

Yes, we were given all these desires, yet it was learning to play the notes at the right time and in the right order that created a perfect melody, the one He had composed. Just because I wore pillowcases on my head as a veil at age six, didn't mean I should have been married at age six. The desire was there, the notes within me even then, but the playing them too early would have ruined the beauty of the song and its intended progression.

I was left with only one question: What tune was I really wanting to play? The tune that everyone else was trying so desperately to play or the one I could create of my own? Perhaps it was one that didn't result in hung corpses on trees, or boyfriends who'd become strangers, nor lying to the two people who were the most important in my life. None of that made music; it made a cacophony of poor choices.

My desire to belong to everyone else had overridden my desire to take care of myself. My need to please others had left me more confused as to who I was than ever before. I knew God had given me the keys, that it was up to me which notes I played. For the first time in what felt like years, I believed I was ready to quiet myself from all the noise of the world around me and hear my own tune. Yet I still did not fully ingest the truth, nor cling to it when things became more tempting. Unfortunately, that glimpse of Him speaking to me became an "If only..." in my life.

In reflection, I only wish I had listened.

CHAPTER 5

Covering Your Bases

Seemingly out of nowhere for a period of time during my teenage years, baseball became vogue at school. Which base people got to was of particular importance, especially with boys and girls who were dating each other. After they hung out the previous evening, the following day would always begin with discussion: "So which base did you guys get to?" It's all anyone ever talked about.

"Second base," I overheard one pupil share.

They're not very good at baseball, I thought. Willie Mays would be very disappointed. I knew little of the sport myself, but at least I knew the aim of the game was to score a home run. Why would someone be proud of only getting to first or second base? It wasn't until I learned that people got naked at third base that I questioned my knowledge of the rules altogether.

Why we created levels for our sexual activity, why we couldn't be clear and call a spade a spade—or in this case, "dry humping"—I'll never know. Perhaps we were making such activities more palatable by attaching them to a sport, which led me to question if we were actually *embarrassed* about our conduct, still a little uncomfortable to say certain words out loud.

I might have been the only one left on the virginity shelf, but the more I stretched the boundaries on physical levels with men, the less resistant to sheepish, "let's do everything but sex" I became. The lines were punch-drunkenly blurred, inspired by peers who didn't know better and provocative pop icons who said being sexual equated to being an adult. I wasn't alone in asking: "How far is too far?" and "When is too soon?" When Oprah aired a show highlighting teenagers who only had anal sex to ensure they were preserving their virginity, I knew we were in trouble. I checked the newspaper to see if it was April Fools—it wasn't. This report was genuine; hundreds of teenagers were kidding themselves in the tomfoolery department of foreplay.

The tension between wanting to be a "satisfactory" girlfriend and looking after my heart was taut. Gone were the days when we had to seek parental permission for our boyfriends to walk us home. Gone were the days when we left kissing on the lips to engagement. Now, getting to date three without noting birthmarks in private places would have been something to brag about. Any faith-led girl lived in a world with consumerist ploys that told her sex was fine as long as she was protected, that sex could fulfill her, even free her.

The Bible was outdated. The old-fashioned warnings of hell and damnation weren't compatible with the all-loving God to whom we were told to devote our lives. "Guilting" people out of sexual discovery was not working. That message didn't come close to provoking the same excitement as Madonna did in her Blonde Ambition tour. We were roused by risk, by anyone who represented strength and liberation. The Church at large was labeled as the repressor of sexuality, made up of control freaks who feared provocative eroticism and the "pleasures of the flesh." Their approach was pushing away the congregation as church members misunderstood the point, thinking Christianity was just another attempt for people to take ownership over our bodies until marriage.

I, too, wasn't immune to skepticism, justifying why it was okay to go *so far* but not *too far*. After all, I wasn't "making babies." It was not "full on" sex. I placed my explorations in the bedroom down to a technicality. I wanted to suggest Christianity's marketing was all wrong, but I didn't have enough knowledge to decide what sexual immorality actually *was*. I was none the wiser. Still I repeated the same irreverent question: "But how far can I go? What can I get away with and still be saved?"

Fumbled answers from the Church would prove useless for my understanding. They said if I was asking that then I was asking the wrong question. I asked what was the right question. They said not to use tongues. I asked where did it say that in the Bible. In fact, didn't it encourage using the gift of tongues? They moved on, telling me to keep an aspirin between my knees. I asked them would Tylenol suffice, as I'm allergic to aspirin. They asked who would want to buy the cow when he already has the milk for free. I folded, wondering how physical endeavors had led us to dairy produce. No one, and I mean *no one*, expounded on the reasons why God made all this for marriage exclusively. Why was everything so full of riddles in church whilst my peers were talking about sex like a game of baseball?

These unanswered musings were creating problems: 1) My experimentation with men and intimacy was making it more difficult to say *no*; and 2) My self-awareness was becoming muddled, more influenced by the people in front of me, less influenced by those who actually cared for me. I dabbled deeper and deeper, exploring the unknown with boyfriends; my friends couldn't understand why I would carry out some sexual activities but never go "all the way." My reasons were falling short of satisfactory, mainly because I didn't fully understand *why* purity was a key message in scripture. What did the Apostle Paul mean when he talked about immorality in the early church? I confess, most of the time when I wasn't in trouble or brave enough to enter Folksworth Church for a mite of conviction, my Bible wasn't used as a life source; it was used as a coffee coaster, a bookend for my chick-lit books. My faith wasn't a relationship; it was a belief I felt far removed from thanks to the postmodern world. Surely something that applied to the first century didn't still apply to the twenty-first? No wonder I was questioning every biblical precept.

All this "you'll get too attached" and "you'll exceed intimacy over trust" was a fair argument, but it still felt fluffy. Interpreted as over-sensitive to the secular world, Christians were still coming across a little wimpy; our overly emotional stance on sex didn't do us any favors.

"You'll get your heart broken" always ruffled the feathers of those who deemed themselves to be thick-skinned, able to handle any challenge, defiant to the end, the "no one can knock me down" types.

"Sex is just sex," they'd say.

Until MRI scans begged to differ.

If faith couldn't give me a good answer, maybe science could, for such research was repudiated to appease skeptics about purity or even God for that matter. As I became fascinated with the joining of science and God, I looked for biological reasons why we should be more mindful in purity. A book called *Hooked* looked at the neuroscience of the brain in physical contact. Hugging for twenty seconds alone moved the chemicals around the synapses, changing the wiring of the brain's neurons. Sexual activity, anything that aroused the body, even without climax, lit the brain up like the dance floor of a seventies discotheque. These chemicals formed attachments—toward a person, toward an act—without needing any moral fiber to make decisions. It's why teenagers loved joy riding; it's why they scored drugs just for the risk: The need for another Dopamine fix (the risk hormone) had them seeking any activity that gave them that high. Oxytocin, the chemical that bonds a mother to her child, releases just as much in sexual conduct *without intercourse.* In short, we were playing Russian roulette with neurons that were meant to build the brain for long-term commitment. The more sex games we played, no matter what bases we reached, the more rewired we got to non-committal relationships, the more addicted we grew to the activity itself instead of the person with whom we were playing. Options grew, patience died, and the desire to serve another became a pre-Bette Davis concept.

Maybe this was why God didn't want us to create false commitments with our bodies. It wasn't a *Hunger Games* challenge to see who could enter Heaven and who'd burn in hell. It was a father telling his kids, "I know *how* you're designed, and you're designed to have sex in a most committed (and therefore most liberal) state. Trust me, I'm suggesting this so that you may experience full joy."

Nobody trusts a person who says he is a vegetarian when he gets caught eating a bacon sandwich on a Sunday morning. No one trusts a dietician who advises cutting out sugar but smokes like Popeye. Hence no one trusted my sentiments anymore when I said I didn't want to lose my virginity before marriage when I was going far enough to have friends tell me idly in conversation, "I find what you did more intimate than sex itself." My pure intentions were starting to become a joke.

Throughout my twenties, I ran to bases like Buster Posey and didn't care that I was an actual *tease.* I found myself only caring for my desires, my needs. That's all it is ever about: *How can I fulfill my needs?* I loathed the men who scoped the room for women who pleased them to the eye, like buying Christian cattle, but my approach to "love" wasn't any more respectable. Attentiveness to the needs of the self was where we were all going wrong. And the irony of all my self-catering? I was losing myself completely. I settled for men who were happy to use me for their own desires, and then I'd be surprised and hurt when they were unkind. Hurt if they showed their true colors with a pocket full of other women's numbers. Hurt if they shared our intimate rendezvous to people I didn't know, uncovering me in their puffed-up glory, shaming me to exalt themselves. These guys didn't care to protect girls, only to tell the world that they were tried-and-true players. The pain and shame I felt over being exposed like this—even without having gone "all the way"—kept me from giving myself totally to any of them. How could I, when I knew the experience wouldn't just belong to us, but to everyone?

In years to come, I'd learn that my friends were right: Some bases are as intimate as intercourse, taking ownership and actually having sex didn't rid me of vulnerability, and it certainly didn't make anything less painful. My intrinsic desire to be with one person, to persevere with one person, to fight through life with one person, to die for one person wasn't influenced by romantic comedies; it was the intention of God, His blueprint for my design. I tried desperately to separate my body from my soul, my head from my heart, but when loss came to town, and when I would have to part with a man I was so pregnant with hope for, I felt like I kept having to deliver unexpected stillbirths.

Three years ago, I moved to California to spend a year at a church and ministry school pursuing Christian spirituality. My faith in God was by this point finally a relationship, one filled with wisdom, fulfillment, self-belief, hope, and inner peace. It was nice, but it didn't make me immune to the sexual wiring I still very much had, now in my early thirties. I found myself in a new environment with men my age, all battling it out for purity this single side of marriage. We had come from some wild walks of life, base attempts and all. My previous experiences weren't quite as colorful as some of my friends', one of whom had earned a living by being a "Butler in the Buff" at bachelorette parties. Another friend had lost her virginity even before puberty; some had even sold their bodies for sex traffickers or loathsome pimps who gave themselves titles like "the devil incarnate." Some had never delved into the journey at all, having happily married young. We had stories and were happy to share when appropriate. But even in my thirties, even when my desire was to wait, to be pure for the sake of my own heart, I still had the same nagging questions from my teenage years: How far *was* too far? How else were we to resolve the sexual frustration we were all facing?

The response to my research brought new revelation. Hell and damnation didn't conclude any argument as it had before. No frown of contempt or pride-fuelled remark bellowed from beneath a bishop's cape. I was introduced to another concept, the one in 1 Corinthians 10:23 that says, "Everything is permissible, but not everything is beneficial." This raised other questions: Maybe it was technically permissible, but just how *beneficial* was going to second base? How healthy was it to tantalize men we respected with our sexuality, yet still hope to keep them from stealing third? I attempted extended kissing in certain relationships, but it was here where I saw the real importance of not running to first base at all.

I kept praying for revelation, for a better understanding, when some guy called Matthew high-fived me in the street.

Matthew 5, came the whisper.

Flicking through to the Sermon on the Mount, I read "To everyone who looks at a woman with lustful intent has already committed adultery with her in his heart" (Matt. 5:28). For your heart's sake, the word *adulterous* does not just define infidelity or unfaithfulness. It's also used for "inconstant," "untrue," and "false-hearted." How tender is the heart that questions, "How much can I get away with and still be saved?" It is inconstant, untrue to the wiring of the brain and the heart; false-hearted for him, false-hearted for her. It lacks true holiness; it lacks God; it feeds us lies about ourselves with which evil wants us to agree.

Even when Christian men edged their way past a safe base and were, at times, disrespecting me, their treatment didn't stem from a lack of love or consideration. They knew when they had pushed too far, even crossing their own physical boundaries. Their shame of dishonoring me eroded their sense of genuine pleasure. You see, within a Christian lifestyle, we're always reaching for a heavenly standard, the one etched before we were born into a world inundated with billboards of nude girls spread over a car hood selling a bottle of Tom Ford perfume.

Teasing, trying so hard to get our needs met sexually, was exactly that: getting needs met. It was not a connection of two people bonding while still being liberal. There was a constant tension around the torturous borders. It wasn't freedom. It was the orchestral equivalent of sitting in the Sydney Opera House, nestled into the seat with a box of Maltesers, dazzled in excitement as the Philharmonic Orchestra begins to play Sergei Rachmaninoff's No.2 in C Minor Op. 18, when, after only twelve bars of music, the conductor grinds everything to a halt and tells the entire audience, "That will be it for this evening." If we can't hear the full symphony, why start playing the dang thing at all?

Within this last year, I was invited to return to my church in England to share my story to a bunch of teenage girls, around fourteen to eighteen years old. That same "but how far…" question was written on pieces of paper and sent my way. I wanted to give them a list of "dos and don'ts," but I knew my fumbled words would just be the same approach as the Church—you know, the explanations that never really answered the question. As I read their thoughts aloud, I felt like a lead balloon had dropped into the room. A crowd of hopeless faces beamed out at me.

They don't need a list, came the voice of my Comforter. *They need hope. They don't even believe in marriage anymore. What would you have told the eighteen-year-old Carrie? Tell them now.*

You could hear a pin drop in the crypt of the church. I once roamed these same rooms wondering whom I could talk to, candidly, about sex. What could I tell that Carrie now? I inhaled a deep breath and braced myself. I didn't really know what might come out of my mouth.

"We all want to meet that special someone. And too often we think we've found him. Too often we believe we've hit the jackpot. Chemicals rush to our head and our loins."

They laughed. A good sign.

"We act on the loins, thinking that they'll make it all better. That once they connect, the boy will be appeased. That we'll be accepted. Sometimes it works. Sometimes people who have sex will go on to have happy, lifelong relationships. But many don't. We never know until we are in that place. Please look at the greater picture. You could have watched *The Fault in our Stars* at the cinema instead of being here tonight. You didn't come here to win a husband or to find a boyfriend. You attend every week with a community that believes in the same thing for the same reason. You came to know God; you came because you believe in a Creator, a Creator who so badly wants to invade your world with His values. Why? Because He loves you. A Dad tells his daughter to be careful to cross the road because he knows the traffic could kill her. But you were too young at four to understand that."

Relationships, never mind marriage, must always begin from a stance of "What can I give this person? What can I bring to the table?" Much of the time, our stance is only found in the sexual experimentation of bedroom antics—running to first, stealing second, teetering between second and third—without self-control, without a hope to build a foundation. I am wired to orgasm, and orgasms, so neuroscience tells me, are as effective for attachment as sex. I was done with attaching myself to men who didn't deserve me in the long run.

Now no one gets the cow's milk. I'm still allergic to aspirin, and kisses remain unknown this side of dating for me personally. Should I wish to enter into a relationship, I will not tease the man with the power of my sexuality. I know not to titillate in fear of being rejected. My relationship with God is too important to pander to little moments in the late hours. And after I raised my standard to ask for nothing but the best in human respect, I found men who refused to lay their hands on me. Men who took ownership of wanting to have their needs met, but were willing to be patient so it didn't harm another, diligent to wait for the bread to fully rise before taking it out of the oven. I found myself shameless after a breakup for the first time when I dated a guy with healthy boundaries. Because of the lack of sexual gratification, he was able to honor me in the separation, without territorial behavior, without any attempts to slander my name due to his own guilt.

I remember the faces of the girls I spoke to in my old church, that new generation of young women who seemed so lost, confused by my life of freedom against the sexualized entrapment of modern day society. They couldn't believe that men could be honorable, that men didn't seek to be loved through the physical, that there were men who refused to lay fingerprints on a woman who wasn't all theirs. Like me, they needed a vision; they needed to interact with men like this. My heartache was that not many men were around them were good examples of selfless love in this particular part of the world. But I hadn't given up hope for them or for me, not just yet. Stewarding my body would prepare a better path to the man who will be so honored, so emotionally touched that I held out for him. Besides, who wants to run from base to base when you could have the entire stadium of Heaven cheering you on when running at the right time to score that home run?

Shameless, full of victory—and naked, of course.

CHAPTER 6

The Conversation

I wanted you to know about me holding out," I told Paul over the phone. "It's only fair to be honest about such things early on." I let out a slightly nervous laugh and waited for his response.

Silence. Quite a bit of it actually.

I met Paul when I was twenty-two during a cheeky little excursion away from working at the busy, exhausting, dirty world of the media industry. We sat next to each other on the plane, both of us flying back home to London from Barcelona. He was 6'4, beautifully dressed, worked in the city, and had muscles with edges so sharp they could cause paper cuts. A two-hour flight was enough to exchange phone numbers and proceed with a few dates in London. After date three, I was back to the place I often found myself when meeting new men, explaining that his burning loins will have to keep on burning, until marriage.

"Well, I wanted to talk to you too," he finally replied. "I've been meaning to say, it's just that…I don't really *do* long distance relationships."

89

He said this flatly, followed by a single cough. He had disconnected quicker than a kid with ADHD being taught arithmetic.

Silence.

"But you live fifteen minutes from me?" I stated bluntly, amused and a little bewildered.

"Well...that's a considerable distance, isn't it?"

"Perhaps," I replied. "If you live in 1913 and don't own a horse."

Needless to say I heard no more from Paul, but I was unaffected. I had come to expect some excuse to be given on why he couldn't see me anymore once I had the "sex talk," or more accurately, the "no sex talk," the one where I indicate—maybe warn—that I wouldn't be having penetrative activity with any man, even handsome ones (something Paul enjoyed talking about) this side of "I do."

Men's responses to this conversation varied from hysterical, spit-out-their-beverage laughter in the assumption I was joking, to large holes in doors, shaped in the outline of the man with whom I had just been sharing sashimi. Some accused me of sexual denial; some suggested I needed to "let myself go;" some asked what I was hiding from or trapping a man into with marriage. But most made excuses so they didn't look quite so moronic for dumping a girl because she wouldn't put out.

The conversation would take different paths of reasoning depending upon the person to whom I was explaining myself. Sometimes I answered with concepts of emotional attachment too often exceeding intimacy. Other times I'd discuss how our culture was inevitably dismantling the *value* of sex with women willing to give themselves for nothing more than a can of Mountain Dew. Men were expected to have sex with any woman with whom they found rapport. So when someone like me came along, a girl with a bit of sass, with a decent quality to her conversation, a guy would have no other go-to but sex. How else could they possibly bond with a girl? It occurred to me that most guys had never been confronted with the question, "Would I wait?" They surprised themselves, not realizing their instinctive behavior.

While the excuses came like clockwork, around the same time and for the same reason, they were never the *same* excuse, which at least kept it interesting. And oh how incredible the imagination was:

"I don't believe in love; therefore I don't believe in marriage."

"I am allergic to conversation."

"What if there is broken glass up there?"

One guy wrote, *You are now married* on a napkin at dinner, turned the napkin toward me, and asked, "What's the difference between that and a marriage certificate?"

"For starters, the law," I sighed.

Men would stand behind me in clubs, repeating: "He's not going to wait for marriage. Neither will he...nor he," while pointing at every single man in the room.

Then there was the usual: "I can't really fall in love unless I can have sex." Such statements were as impressive as a man telling me he can't swim without floaties.

I see, I always thought to myself. Yes, I understand about neurological bonding. Yes, I get the legitimate desire to connect physically when there is serious attraction or even slight mutual interest.

But how can a man possibly fall in love without sex? The same way he can fall *out* of love, even when he's having loads of it. It isn't the compatible sex that pushes the man away, but rather the lack of respect, the crap chat, the inability to have a sense of humor, the bad spending habits, or that a girl simply can't be trusted.

Do not misunderstand me. I wasn't using the concept of abstinence as if it were some kind of mind game, the ultimate test of triumph for the burning-loin brigade. No. My heart to value myself, to not give all the candy away, was becoming more supported by these continuous, non-stop discussions that led me to question if men thought outside of the boudoir.

Instead of having these disheartening dialogues all the time, some girlfriends took the liberty to pass on the information about my no-sex decisions like a weather warning. Even with guys I fancied, so bored I was with the same conversation, I gave permission for the girls who loved me to take it upon themselves and explain the theory of "Carrie's chastity." I would overhear them milk the explanation, scaring some men on purpose, not for competitive reasons in obtaining him for themselves, but because the caliber of gent was so appalling, so about their own obvious desires to have sex, to "love" and leave. My girls would warn men off the way one might ward off vampires, using the word *Jesus* as the crucifix equivalent.

"What? She doesn't have sex? Like…no sex?" some drunkard would inquire.

"Oh, no, no," my friend would nonchalantly share. "Carrie might spontaneously combust if she had sex before marriage, a bit like Cinderella and her carriage turning into a pumpkin after midnight. It's all in the timing for her. Yes. One time, when she was dating this actor, she went a little close to the bone—no pun intended—and the electrics in the house began to flash on and off. Then her hand caught fire. I can't even go into what happened to the guy's doodah."

While the electrical happenings might have been just a bit exaggerated, the actor was not. He had been in London's *Blood Brothers*. While we were dating, he would travel seven hours on a bus from London to Liverpool—how's that for "long distance"—and stock my fridge with food (student living lacked such luxuries as a full fridge). One day he left a note on the counter: "I love you so much. P.S. Most people would be having sex by now."

Like clockwork.

My friends would typically end these explanations with something like: "But she's cool. Jesus really likes her. If you want, she'll put in a good word for you."

Eventually, I considered going for the older man, hoping to find someone who had gone around the sexual block, happy to wait for a little more than a physical union on a Tempur-Pedic mattress. For him to believe in God would have been nice too, but judging the environment I lived in, not one man had faith. If I did manage to bring up faith as part of my reason to abstain, some would laugh, finish their pint, and end with, "Well it was nice talking to you...perhaps I could introduce you to my brother? His name is Batman."

Before long, I began to feel like my reasons for holding out for my wedding night were becoming a little jaded. Was I completely insane? I had no Christian community to remind me of why purity protects the soul instead of draining it. The stark commentary I received every day made it apparent I may never marry if I didn't have sex.

Perhaps I was going about this whole thing the wrong way. I needed to stop looking for someone who would wait for me. Just like my virgin-heroine plays at age fifteen, I needed some leverage that made it socially acceptable, even appropriate, for me to hold out.

Mother Teresa had a different focus. *Yes, that's it*, I thought to myself, *I'll get a career. Then when I'm rich, or a saint, people will wait for as long as I tell them to.*

The film industry was my vocation of choice, and in my last year of university I leapt at the chance to be a club dancer in a potential blockbuster. The movie starred one of my acting heroes, Samuel L. Jackson, along with a few other prolific names I had read about but never met in the flesh. Being a film extra was an odd method to becoming a successful actress, but it was the only shot I had and a foot in the door. On Day Two of filming, the director's assistant came up to me, clipboard in hand.

"Hi there. The director wanted me to take your details. I'm his assistant, Max. He wondered if he could contact you?"

"Sure." I caught the director's eye, watching me pass on my number. He smiled at me from his chair behind the cameras.

I was confused, naturally, as I had been picked out from one hundred and twenty extras on set. Maybe my leap to fame and riches wouldn't take quite so long after all. The following day I was invited to dinner with the director and his crew. I arrived at a restaurant with him and five other gentleman in their fifties. The director had quite the filmography, with many movies becoming household names. I wasn't sure why I had been invited, seeing as I was a lowly extra, but it wasn't the only invitation extended my way. He asked me to join him at restaurants during the evenings. I'd attend exclusive parties as his plus one. I got to sit on set while he worked. My life had turned into a bonkers storyline at only twenty-two. I called this the golden era: a period of intense favor with brilliant supper stories to match.

He was very accommodating. When he asked if I had watched any of his films, I apologized and confessed I hadn't, mainly because I didn't have a DVD player. The next day my doorbell rang with a very rained-on Max, holding a brand new DVD player and a box set of the director's films. All of this without any hint of something being required from me. Never did he make a move or do anything that was untoward.

Perhaps I had finally found *him*, a man who could be a friend, someone who had clean intentions. Younger men might have wanted to do things to me, but older men wanted to protect me.

Or so I thought.

At the wrap party after three months of shooting, I sat with the director all evening. We were discussing my next moves and desire to be an actress. Not only had I met a man who didn't pressure to me have sex in exchange for his attention, I met someone who actually wanted to help me with my career—someone who actually *could* help me. Of course I wanted him to screen test me, to see my ability to act, but just as I didn't want to be taken advantage of, neither did I want to take advantage of his prowess in the film industry.

"Let me ask you something, Carrie." He scooped himself up closer to me on the sofa so that only I could hear him. "Imagine: You're in L.A. You've met a director who can give you the world, can give you the spotlight. And he turns to you, saying, 'I'll give you the greatest role I have to offer...if you sleep with me tonight.' What would you do?"

I looked around to see if I was on set of *Indecent Proposal*, but Robert Redford was nowhere to be seen. My stomach dropped. Concerned this was a passive dig to see my true intentions or a sly move to see if I would sleep with a director, I swallowed my breath. "I'd like to think that Judi Dench had enough talent to bypass any duty to sleep with a director. I'd like to think that should I find myself under movie set spotlights, I'd not have to think, *I'm here for all the wrong reasons*. Nope. I wouldn't do it. I'd only sleep with a director if he was my man—more importantly, my husband."

His weak smile showed traces of hopelessness. He continued sitting next to me for another hour, but his gaze fell on the shrimp crudités. No amount of time spent with men made my choices any more comprehensible, it seemed. They could decide I was Goldie Hawn herself, they could wine and dine me until Kurt Russell came home, but the fact remained, I was still unable to give them what they wanted, and they were unwilling to give me what I longed for.

Of course, I make recounting these stories sound easy, as if I were living on the higher road, above such meaningless intentions. As if I didn't want to engage in sex nor have anything to do with it. As if I were riddled with a prudish attitude that disdained the entire idea of skin-on-skin contact. Of course not. I simply refused to make how we connected to another through sex be the defining factor of my relationship. I wanted it to be an additional bonus from committing to someone. I was merely sifting the wheat from the chaff. Problem was, I was still yet to find any wheat.

Not before long, my defense for the case became so intrinsic that I was one day away from getting an actual soapbox, campaigning for chastity like I would for a female president. "And another thing!" I'd argue on my nights out. "When people in meaningful relationships talk about it, how often do you hear them say, 'It's far more than sex. She gets me, she understands me, she's funny, and she…'? When couples get engaged, they stop having sex for a duration of time, hoping to make their wedding night *special*. Subconsciously, we all want to be exclusive to one, not one amongst a bigger number. But is anyone willing to have a little patience? OH NO! We have to mount everything that moves these days. Why don't I just hump this bar stool and rejoice in my freedom!?" My entire face would turn crimson as spectators' eyes widened.

Some unfortunate man might walk up to me at a bar to start a conversation, and before he knew it, he had embarked on a mental bus tour of my brain. No one needed to see me in the eye of this storm, believe me.

"Before succumbing to the very real desires we all have in sex, why don't we learn details of a person? Hmm?" I'd harp on. "The sense of humor, the likes, the dislikes, the appreciation of a person's soul before their body, searching for an *ounce* of respect, a *teaspoon* of emotional connection with a desire to serve each other as friends as well as lovers.

If we pander to every desire, that's when affairs happen, people file for bankruptcy, prostitutes face abuse, Gonorrhea gets contracted, sex-trafficking becomes an industry, drugs feed the addict, and we are more trapped in hell than ever before."

"Excuse me, but I was just wanting to know if you're waiting to be served at the bar?" one guy asked.

"Oh…No. I've got my lemonade, thanks." In order to maintain a scrap of dignity from my long rant, I left him with: "Besides, you'll probably spike my drink with Rohypnol." Then, of course, I saw his wife is standing next to him, staring at me as perplexed as I was.

Such was the bizarre perspective I was slowly creating, a lens full of fear, poor judgment, irrationality, and bullet points ready to fight my own ground. And the truth was…I had become exhausted. When faced with the same question over and over, I was finished with explaining why not having sex was more loving and more honorable outside of commitment— of which marriage was the ultimate, hopefully final act. Before that, one could get a refund. I was tired of being seen as a fairytale believer, a naïve idealist. Most people in generations before never had to have these conversations. What had happened in the world for abstinence to make a girl a freak of society?

Did I wish I were more accepted in the world I lived in? Absolutely. My friends not only accepted me, they defended me often at times, reveling in my differences. But there was always an urge to be understood by *men*, to be seen as a real woman, one who held not just her own in this war of the words I frequented on, but as a girl who longed for intimacy and chemistry with males. In time, I learned my lesson, knowing defense was an ugly reaction. I didn't need to waste any more time trying to fight a losing battle. You can only try to explain yourself for so long. All I wanted was someone to be willing to go the long distance, more than the fifteen minutes Paul and the like could give.

As demoralizing and entertaining as these conversations were, the hula-hoop of discussion only made me yearn for some male protection, something that even vaguely resembled the kind I only got in a fatherly manner at home. I finally gave up my weapons of defense and logical arguments and trusted I may meet another man like me one day, or one who at least understood. Why did I need to explain myself to people who didn't care about God anyway? Why was I expecting heavenly concepts to be embraced by people who didn't embrace Heaven itself?

In the meantime I decided to use the get-out-of-jail card my friends—in all their wisdom—had given me: "Why don't I have sex, you ask? Well, for one, I might burst into flames if I try before I'm a bride. Strange things start to happen when I get too close, so it's just best I don't."

"Now if you'll excuse me, my Batmobile awaits."

CHAPTER 7

Daddy's Girl

When I turned eighteen, Dad underwent a serious heart operation so severe it nearly killed him. It left him with some brain damage, and he exited the hospital as a very different person than the one who entered. An administration of too high a dose of morphine took away his capacity to have control in certain areas of his life and behavior. He began to sterilize his life with alcohol after a doctor suggested he should "take a couple of sherries before bed time" to help his insomniatic suffering. The doctor could not have known it would turn into a disruptive bi-weekly habit that slowly became a regular walk down misery lane.

Overnight my father, the man who had taken ecstatic joy in a risk-taking life, the man who so beautifully built a sense of worth in me in my formative years, became unable to protect me from his own inner fear-ridden dialogue. He became unhealthy with the drink, not everyday, but I would find him asleep for a day or two, using his new friend to help ease the pain.

The roles began to reverse as Dad clung onto my leg, saying, "I'm not well, Carrie. I'm not well."

I'd cry into him, Mum finding us in a heap on the floor. Other days I'd be angry, having little compassion for addiction. I wanted to fix it all and fight for him after everything he had done for me. The concoction of emotions went from bitterness to deep sadness, from hope after six months of sobriety to despair during his relapses.

The value Dad so often placed in me felt secondary to liquor even though he was brilliantly honest in his addictive journey. I questioned having a secondhand faith through a parent who was struggling with his own demons. In our times of strife, hopelessness took over, and even in the loose relationship I had with God, my cryings-out felt like echoed shouts in empty tunnels—with no response. For me, seeing my preacher papa enter into substance abuse caused me to question everything he taught. What happened to relying on God? What happened to Him being our refuge? Perhaps the Bible was more outdated than I had thought.

It was here, amid my weakening strength, when I met a twenty-three year-old Muslim, RoRo, a man who said he'd actually *wait* for me until marriage and meant it. You can imagine my jaw-dropping astonishment. His arrival, his acceptance of who I was broke down my walls like trumpets over the ancient walls of Jericho. He utterly adored me. Across rooms, he'd stare at me; I'd catch him out, but unashamedly he kept watching, and I liked it. He'd do anything for me, fight for me, comfort me, and connect in ways I'd not had for a while. Such unconditional love removed the pin from this dusty grenade…

My justification for purity had been buried over the years with my boundaries in previous relationships being stretched like socks. They never retorted back to their usual shape—surely it was only a matter of *when*. All that white knuckling had been eradicated from a man who told me he would wait, and so I broke, assuming sex was where I'd find respite from my grief, my disappointment in my father, and ultimately in God. Here I lost my virginity without any planned intention. I fell into the boring, cliché "it just happened" bracket. I was no victim to temptation. I simply lost hope for why I should wait. We were going to marry anyway. I loved him; he loved me.

The feeling of fulfillment didn't last long. I lived in a fog for months, repeating the same action, all the while mourning the fact that I had fought the battlefield of virginity for so long only to give in to sex this way. It was at this point in my life where FOMO, the fear of missing out, really came to town: when I couldn't hear God any more.

I'd speak to Him but get no response. Not like before. Unlike the times in which I could almost tangibly touch His presence, now I'd sense nothing but empty air. I'd walk around in a daze of conviction, thinking, "I've messed with my Dad, and he's not talking to me." Of course this wasn't the case. God hadn't packed up and left my apartment block. Misplacing my sexuality didn't mean I was going directly to the burning pit of hell. I had simply come into agreement with something that wasn't peaceful. My fight for purity was eroded the moment I couldn't find a reason to continue.

I thought I'd be free?

I was confused as to why everyone wanted me to lose my virginity, when sex really was just sex. I didn't feel like swinging from the lampshades nor burning my bras along some country lane in Wales. I was no wiser; I wasn't automatically better at math or even biology. Sex was pleasant, jubilant, and euphoric for a few moments, and then I was back to Planet Earth, still without a solid understanding of black holes.

One thing I did know: the teasing from kids, the hostility from the mob mentality certainly didn't match the experience of sex. It didn't warrant snide remarks or isolation. Sex was an adult game, played too often by children. Even at twenty-three, I still felt like I had entered a bar under age, unable to hold my liquor.

RoRo had a large family that attempted to pitch him to Pakistani women every summer abroad. Adorned females were shoved toward him in the streets, while images of him finding "the one" kept barraging my mind at home. When the family saw their methods of arranged marriage weren't working, they wanted me to become Muslim, which proved a little tricky for my, albeit fragile, belief in Christianity. No matter how earth-shattering the physical side might have been, no bond could keep out the problem areas of our relationship. They could mask it for a while, but it couldn't solve the very real issues we faced. We tried to make it work, but I knew I'd lose the essence of who I was—I knew I couldn't truly convert. I ended the relationship, broke his heart, which in turn broke mine.

Attempting to suffocate my real emotions, I moved to London to work for one of the all-time greats in casting direction. A marvelous job I maintained for three months…until the rage, the telephones thrown at my head, and the inappropriate text messages sent to me at 4:00 a.m., suggesting what one of the directors wanted to do to me. I declined a full-time contract and moved back home. I was running away from the intimacy I had created with a man I never ended up being with forever, ashamed that I couldn't have just waited. In his mourning, just like I hid my head in the workplace sand, he slept with other women, confessing it to me, breaking their hearts and mine all over again. Sex had become his comfort blanket.

Like clockwork, after a six-month spate of sobriety, my father relapsed. I had waited five years to speak up about how hurtful it was seeing Dad this way; I wanted the old Dad back. I chose the wrong time to confront, however, and was asked to leave the house, to find somewhere else to live that very night. For three weeks I surfed my mate's sofas, attending open Alcoholics Anonymous meetings, trying to get my head around the addict's psychosis. Did the addict love us still, despite letting, even helplessly, this substance break connection with us? Fathers and mothers in this meeting all felt they had wrecked not only their own lives, but also their children's. I had become obsessed with wanting to help Pops, and in response, lost myself even more by trying to control a situation that was out of my hands.

Because I couldn't manage the pain of breaking RoRo's heart, because I had nowhere to be comforted in Stamford, I fled back to London, working fifteen-hour days. I found a man named Otto whom I thought was wonderful, perhaps more suited in values than my ex. Both of us were creative, both Christians. At twenty-three, we were still on that identity slump—needing to chase dreams even though we weren't sure what they were. A proper job, even one that paid well, that didn't involve *fun* was a lethal thought. We travelled Europe for a little while on no budget, camping under the stars on Tavira's beaches. But eventually I had to get back to "real life," as I was supporting myself without my parents' help.

When I was offered a role in magazine publishing, the one person I wanted to call to invite the usual cheerleading escapade on any achievement I had, was the last person I could muster humility for. When I did call for Mum, Dad tried to take the phone to talk to me. I hung up before he got to hear my voice. I couldn't pretend everything was fine. It wasn't. We had been carrying out some sort of pantomime with flamingo-colored elephants in the room for two years. I found temporary release by crying on the shoulders of friends and my boyfriend. But nothing resolved my pain.

Saturday would be the day a phone call changed my life. Something isn't good when a complete stranger calls from your home phone, asking for you to call urgently. I was driving to London with Otto for a birthday party, busting tunes that perforated my eardrums. On hearing the voicemail, I asked him to pull over. I waited outside of the car for Otto to call my home. His face dropped, his head on the steering wheel. He got out of the car, a tear rolling down his face.

"Your father passed away this afternoon."

All sound stopped on the motorway. It must have been some sick joke. I remember smiling because it wasn't real. I called my mother, but the police were interviewing her.

I u-turned and drove back to Lincolnshire. Crying in disbelief, returning to an empty house where my father's booming voice was now missing, the place noiseless but for the sniffles of a bereaved wife. The laughter, the running around, our recreation of the sword fights in *Hamlet* were now haunting memories in my home. My belief in religion felt like a ghostly science; my hurt over losing him rendered me screaming in fields, begging whomever God was to bring him back.

No goodbye, no chance for love notes, no chance to amend the only argument we'd ever had in our entire relationship. The man who fought for me in the streets had now been carted out of my house into a body bag, refrigerated in a morgue.

There was a cold silence on seeing my mother. I forgot that Dad didn't just take care of me, he took care of both of us, regardless of his pain.

She stared at me in a solemn grief that was foreign.

I had nothing, no words, no understanding. Shock dumbed me.

In the silence, she managed to muster a sentence. "He'd watch you for hours as a baby, not believing you could be his. That never changed. You do know that, don't you?" Her brilliance of grabbing the jugular and confronting the greatest fear I had always cut to my core. The falling out Dad and I had in recent weeks was trivial compared to death. I thought I was helping by not succumbing, by not pretending his relapse was fine.

"But...but...did he know I loved him too?" I asked in an eight-year old's feeble voice. I collapsed to the floor, my mother instinctively wanting to comfort me. Instead, she stared into the dark, hiccupping for breath, empty and undone.

The coffin arrived at our home; the hearse and limo jaguars lined the streets. Bikers from the 1960s, men who were members of the Suzuki Owner's Club, a club that Dad co-founded with a bunch of Hell's Angels in 1968, arrived. I went to shake their hands; they nodded in solemnity. The pain of losing him was deep for many. As I walked back to my seat in the jaguar, I turned to see their wreath leaning against Dad's coffin: a red, "S"-shaped arrangement with a note that read, "Without whom we wouldn't be here." I forgot about the lives he saved before I was born, pulling men off the streets, dragging them from violence and murder in Manchester, teaching them about the wonder of God and the wonder of a motorcycle. Death couldn't defeat our love for him.

As the coffin stood in front of me in the church amid a sea of black, the hymns began and thoughts infiltrated my concentration. My first ever memory of Dad at gunpoint on the inner German border, shouting over my four-year-old screams to my mother: "Get Carrie out of here!" Pops had travelled to East Germany to smuggle Bibles and see his friends, but had been mistaken for someone else. I was so attached to him even at four; watching him under threat by German soldiers destroyed me. I had been scared of losing him ever since.

No matter what circumstance I faced with my rather adventurous, Bible-smuggling parents, I never assumed for a minute that we'd be harmed—Gamma gun to the temple or not. Yet here I was, seeing his coffin at an age when my own independent life hadn't even begun.

Fifteen minutes into the ceremony and the flowers on the coffin began to shake. My boyfriend's little brother and I stopped singing to see what was making them move. Suddenly, a white butterfly crawled out from the flowers, taking flight over our heads and spiraling upward into the steeple of the church. People began to break down in tears, but my shock was too rife for me to express any emotion. I took note of the butterfly, but it would be another five years before I learned what it meant.

The hearse now empty, the funeral director in tails and a top hat. I walked with him along the path; he'd been a great comfort to me, by my side when identifying the body and here, walking in procession of the coffin.

"Who else did you have to bury today?" I asked him.

"Twins." He looked at me with sorrow. "The mother jumped into the grave with them, wailing in denial."

Death was an odious thing. I couldn't comprehend the pain of a mother watching her child die, especially if it felt this excruciating for the natural order, my Dad dying in a humanely "swift" way. I looked up at the sky, at the church's cross, another ugly symbol to remind me of one more man's death, ten years older than I, his brothers, sisters, and mother forced to watch the most brutal murder imaginable.

Cards from around the world kept my mother and I occupied. Grief was a consuming emotion. I took care of the house with mum, due to financial difficulties with Dad's death. Responsibility came upon us overnight, and although I needed friends, no one knew this pain unless they had gone through it as well. Only fellow widowers or parentless friends were able to help, though even many of these were unsure about what to say if they saw me approach.

Because of Dad's sudden death, my new job had to be postponed. He had died two days before my new career in magazines was to start. Mum confessed that Dad had intended to send flowers on my first day. But four days after the funeral, there were no flowers on my new desk, just a computer and a newly dated contract saying that my company was not going to pay for those first two weeks of grievance. As if it were some sort of holiday for me. Oh how brutal the business world can be.

In adjusting to a new life without Dad, I sought to find father figures around me: my mum's brother who always made me giggle and gave great strength to my mother; my uncle David, Dad's brother, who lived on Redondo Beach in Los Angeles. Otto and I flew to visit David for a week, and my heart was comforted, knowing that there was one other male Lloyd left in the family. But he soon disclosed that his Leukemia only gave him months to live. Not wanting to miss a moment, I couldn't stop telling him I loved him, and when I left, I ran back into his apartment to hug him—just in case it was the last time.

All this grief made my boyfriend desperate for attention. He rarely understood why I needed to focus on my mother or my sorrow. The jealousy made me feel more under attack. When all I could think about was the massive hole that only the dead returned could fill, being misjudged by someone I wanted connection with felt even more soul destroying.

He ended the relationship during the flight back from L.A., conveying the news by writing it on a napkin and passing it via the person sitting between us. I was left solo to collect my Samsonite in Heathrow's baggage claim. I'd never felt more alone, and wondered if perhaps my father was the only one who would ever want to fight through the hard times with me. On top of everything, I returned home and received yet another phone call giving me a blow. Uncle David had died.

Four more people died within eighteen months: my mum's brother, two male friends on separate motorbike accidents, and my auntie. Death had stolen my hope; pain ate at my insides; smoking cigarettes was a momentary comfort, while prayer felt like painful nothings spoken to jacquard wallpaper. Desperate, I asked God to show me who He was, to fill the room with a presence that I couldn't ignore. I waited for an hour in the silence. The sun had set, and the light faded from the window to flood the room into complete darkness, yet I still knelt there. Hoping for some light. Hoping for the whisper—but nothing came.

I was done. I decided to put my faith out that night with the trash once and for all. How could I be faced with this torment and not be given one ounce of hope, a flicker of light, a whisper of wisdom? I left God and went in search for the new atheism, one filled with logic, bitterness, and a bee-filled bonnet.

Otto reconnected with me a couple of months later, asking to meet in a hotel for an evening. Even though I had never had sex with him, we made out—some bizarre move on my part, hoping he'd come back to me. He chose another public place to tell me we wouldn't be getting back together, that he wanted to be happy. I guess it was kind of him to verbally share this time, instead of scribbling it on a napkin.

Now I was mad at God *and* men. I couldn't face the loneliness or the sense of abandonment anymore. I shoved my bereavement to a pocket in my brain, with the world unable to handle me in pain; any form of vulnerability about the subject left me more sensitive to people's insensitive actions.

Was losing my virginity a response to my broken need to be loved when I felt like my entire world (my dad) was being snatched away from me? Was it because I no longer had anyone to value myself for? The roller coaster relationship I had with my father at the very end had a direct correlation with men. As long as I was getting value from him, all was fine; I knew why I should take care of myself: My father loved me. But after his death, I became a sucker to the lie that said giving my entire being to a man who "was different" would finally scratch my "need to give a man satisfaction" itch.

Oh, there were some arguments to appease my decision: "But you loved him; you're an adult; you were responsible and on contraception, so what's the problem? There's too much shame on you, Carrie." Still, I couldn't explain why, especially now I had no spiritual reasoning to hold out, I felt I should have waited. Why didn't I wait with RoRo? One thing I did know is that although I loved him, I took something from him, some mystery, and I leant him mine. I never wanted to lend him anything, nothing was meant to be *on loan*. I wasn't some sexual pawnbroker. I wanted him to have me forever, to keep what I offered. I didn't expect returns. I knew this could end in tears without the ultimate commitment, and yet I set my heart and body up for it, not knowing just how utterly painful it would be. When it came to losing my father, Otto couldn't, understandably at the age of twenty-four, love me through that process. Fear overrode love because Otto didn't have the answers and couldn't make me better again. With so much death chasing my family, I too was suffocating in the stuff.

Orphaned by death and by men's choices, I didn't walk in a sense of security; I crawled with a lack of hope, a lack of value, and a fear of losing everything. That's never a place anyone wants to be, and yet when I looked around my acquaintances, so many were running in fear of something, of some pain, of some lie that the world was crap and didn't care about whether they'd find a happy ending.

Although Hitchens, Dawkins, McGrath had unknowingly become my best friends through their books, that desire to love and be loved in abundance kept hounding me. Science couldn't answer it. Yes, we have chemicals that forge and create love bonds, but why were they there in the first place? Why were they even in the human form? What would be the point of having humans and creation with feelings and emotions if there is no point to existence at all? I wasn't here to just procreate, surely. No man wants to fly to the moon, to explore and expand for no reason. C.S. Lewis talked of the four loves: Eros, Philia, Storge, and Agape. Why have any of those if there is no purpose for them?

As I started this new subconscious board game of hurting others—a side effect of handling other people's reckless actions, I became unrecognizable to myself. Not only was I snowballing toward more futile endings, I was gaining a momentum that not even the finest of God's angels could have stopped.

CHAPTER 8

The Decadent Days

2007. 3:00 a.m. An original light saber from the set of *Star Wars* in one hand, glass of Krug in the other, chasing my potential new boss around his skyline apartment. I say *potential boss* because this interesting turn of events just so happened to be my job interview. Spartacus, or Sparty to you and me, was looking for his 36th executive assistant since he started as Creative Director to one of the top advertising agencies in the world one year prior. Most of his assistants couldn't survive twenty-four hours and left before he had the chance to throw a computer at them. That, or he found them too boring, and so, threw a computer at them. *Devil Wear Prada's* Miranda Priestly, the infamous "ice queen," was a ragdoll kitten compared to this viper. Yet, now in my late twenties, I was unfazed by such reports because I needed a job after acquiring a brand new mortgage with just £21.43 in my bank account.

I kept swinging the light saber like a baseball bat, normally mounted next to an original Gavin Turk (whoever on earth Gavin Turk was), squinting one eye as I took aim for a shoe I'd placed on his head. He smiled, appreciating the cockiness of this twenty-seven year old toward a fifty-something man. He was tall, dyed his hair to mask his age, sharply dressed, and had a slight lisp. His apartment was the most sought after address in southeast London (a glorious side effect of being famous in advertising), he had never married, always requested for a limo to take him from Beak Street to Oxford street (that's 150 yards), and hated puns. He was, oddly, quite sexy in a powerful kind of way. Women flocked to him, men wanted his approval, and his tailor was John Pearse, the tailor to the stars, the godfather of tailors to the bespoke casual.

I had planned to stay at my friend's house that evening, but the interview had gone on longer than anticipated, mainly because a random stranger from across the bar, Twig, the same man who ended up buying me the bottle of Krug that began my evening demise, had a strange star-struck moment with Sparty and wouldn't leave him (and therefore me) alone. Sparty's attention waned with the lack of copious cocaine offers, while Twig's three-piece pinstripe suit with matching monocle wasn't working for me either.

"You don't remember me, do you? After all these years, I'd thought you'd remember me. Especially after—"

"Twig, I do remember you, but you're spitting into my retina." Sparty sighed.

"Sorry. Sorry mate, I'll leave you with your girlfriend."

"She's not my girlfriend."

"You want a line?" Twig asked, turning to me.

"No, you're good thanks," I sheepishly replied.

"Just a little one?" as if he were asking about a French fry.

"No....really, I—"

"Just a little tinsy one?"

I blurted out, "I'm allergic to aspirin."

Silence fell, both Twig and Sparty dropped jaws, and I swear the pianist in the lounge jumped the wrong chord too.

Sparty began laughing: "To get ahead in advertising you're going to need a little coke, babe."

When I took the job, advertising did not come with a health warning, nor did I imagine I'd hear stories of my boss standing on the Millennium Bridge at 12:30 a.m. with a live Boa Constrictor around his neck reciting a poem about courage to a new starter at the agency. But this was my life now. The white marbled agency that turned over 120 million a year contained some of the greatest creative brains on the planet with some of the original "Mad Men" to match. The TV show depicting the ad execs on Madison Avenue had nothing on the real life version though. The marriages never lasted, drugs were like *aperitifs* before breakfast, and the story of an advertising production team flying a helicopter over an amazon forest on too much vodka was actually true. When the chopper nearly crashed twelve nervous execs, clients, and producers into a mountain, one would be correct to guess it was the account director who claimed, amidst the screams of hilarity and panic: "From now on, only the *pilots* get to operate the helicopter!" before downing another shot.

I'm not sure when I gauged how barbaric my life had become in order to achieve a reputable career. Maybe it was the time I found a piece of paper on Sparty's desk with the words: "I am more powerful than the Solar System" in his handwriting. I couldn't work out if this was a tagline for an advert or the daily affirmation by Sparty, for Sparty. That I had to question it at all alerted me to the beautiful creativity that could emerge from narcissism. I enjoyed the fearlessness of the ego. I reveled in the insane hilarity of it all, until it fell into physical fighting—another moment when I realized the rules really were different when someone is paid a fortune to run a think tank. On one occasion I could see through the glass a few offices down from Sparky's that two creatives were holding each other by the throat.

"What is going on with Stu and Andrew?!" I asked.

"They've been at it for about thirty minutes," Sparty answered without looking up. He sipped his cup of tea, then grimaced: "Carrie, did you leave this tea bag in to stew for a minute and then take it out? Or did you squidge the tea bag against the side of the mug and then take it out?"

"Squidged it," I said, still wincing at the fisticuffs taking place five doors down.

"You've ruined it. It's perfectly simple—"

"Boss, I think you should be aware that Stu's tooth has just come out against the glass wall."

Although Sparty was eye level to the action in hand, he was much more perturbed by my appalling tea-making skills. "I'm going to make a paint test strip so you know exactly what color I need my tea to be. I'll tattoo on your hand that you must not squidge the bag against the cup. And leave those two. They create better work when they bleed. Or in this case, lose teeth."

I was surrounded by the most reputable people in the advertising world, both for their genius ideas and for their debauched behavior. At least one of the teams was always flying to New York every month to collect an award, and every other month we had the finest of artists in their crafts talk to our twenty-strong team. Comedy writer Armando Lannucci, famous for shows like *The Thick of It* and *In the Loop*, and I would have probably become friends if I had only known how to work the DVD player to accompany his talk. Instead he was pretty cross with me—and the DVD player. Famous film directors David Puttnam and Ridley Scott waltzed onto the creative floor, which was sprinkled with urban street artists hosting massive events with or without Banksy.

The more weirdly individual you were, the more praised you were. Tracey Emin and Marina Abramovic, the Serbian performance artist, were heralded to a state of creative sainthood. I'd view the famous *Bed* piece by Tracey Emin in the Saatchi Gallery, turn my nose up, and say, "It's still implausible to me. I mean, it's hardly a Rembrandt, is it?"

"I think it's a masterpiece," Sparty would retort.

The industry was still male heavy, hedonistic, and purposely politically incorrect. Department meetings were filled with testosterone-weighted sexual innuendo and competitive arrogance brasher than Prime Minister question time. Before Sparty was appointed, the daily agenda for the creative floor entailed daylong sessions of poker, smoking, cocaine ingesting like a kid with sherbet, drinking around the clock, and little sleep. The work got done when the deadline loomed, but most of the inspiration came from current tabloids and ad land gossip. Somehow the work was still decent, even brilliant. Their brains were wired to be different from the rest of us. Most would say hanging actors upside down on set for better performances would be abusive, but in advertising, it was the work of a directorial genius, and my, what a difference a trapeze makes.

The opulence was energetic, vibrant, liberal, exhilarating, chaotic, contagiously venomous, self-seeking, boastful, out of control, and so cutthroat I cried seven times a day in the toilet. I was a sensitive bean, and although I tried to play the game (allergies to cocaine aside), I was unable to manage the hot-and-cold treatment. One day I was a legend, the next I was as useful as a dead dog. Because I based my identity on my career as well as the approval of male mentors, heroes to me at this time, waterproof mascara was a necessity. Our days often ended at 2:00 a.m. to be ready for an 8:00 a.m. start. Advertising was our oxygen, and we were to know who had power versus who just ruined their reputation based on one thirty-second commercial.

Whom we befriended was purely about connections, not the person behind it. I had killer connections, but how empty it all felt. I only wined and dined for rapacious reasons. Like a celebrity blinded by cameras, we all felt unknown, living a professional pantomime. Beyond the parked Bentleys, I did have some consistency in my life, thanks to Caleb, my new man. Clichéd in his tall, dark, handsome appearance, Caleb was a producer in television who had invented a fictitious need for me to edit a show reel for him, then on my acceptance told me the edit suite was no longer available, but would I like a nice glass of Chianti? This was the beginning of our five-year relationship. Women weren't happy he was off the market; Sparty was also displeased with this new distraction from my twenty-five hour workdays. And like all decent guys, Caleb didn't want to fight for time between Sparty and me. You could cut the air with Sparty's samurai sword, which sat mounted next to his taxidermied cat, should they be in the same room together.

Any relationship that entailed monogamy was odd compared to the temporary unions that frequented the dark streets of Soho. My relationship with Caleb wasn't deemed "cool" to the media dimension, knowing we would have excelled further had we been single. But this was a done deal. There was no one else I wanted, and due to our emotional connection, the physical followed very quickly. We'd travel to work together using the escalators to stand and kiss, lunch breaks to stare at each other, evenings to talk and fall further in love. He was perfect.

Kind.

Dedicated.

Humorously naughty.

For a time all was jubilant, but home eventually became a dungeon of bitter roommates who formed a bizarre gang mentality against my newly found happiness in love. Work was burning me out, and the girls at the office wouldn't let go of Caleb being taken. I lost weight faster than an avid Atkins dieter would approve, and the anxiety robbed me of sleep. Caleb and I were cast out of our social networks. I was no longer a legend at work (the "new girl" label only lasted so long), and I became my co-workers' pincushion when they needed to blame someone if they made a mistake. People weren't afraid to tell you they hated you. My daily journey to work made me nauseous and fearful.

After a year, I was offered another job by a production company, and I jumped ship, deciding the production side of advertising might be a better fit—I mean, *anything* would have been better at this point. I loved it, but my body had already taken a beating: Stomach pains increased, I was thirty pounds down in weight, and I could barely keep my head up in meetings. Some nights I'd collapse without being able to call down to those I lived with, which wouldn't have helped anyway since they barely talked to me. Blood tests were taken between meetings; potential chronic fatigue, parasites, ovarian problems were all on the table. Doctors could not explain why I wanted to puke into my Marc Jacobs handbag every hour. Within a few weeks of my new job, I was bedridden, frail, and almost unable to walk. When it came to London careers, if you weren't working after four weeks, someone had to take over your job, as well as your accommodation. I was replaced both in the office and in my flat.

I moved back home at twenty-nine, depressed, totally deprived of ego. Unlike in the advertising world where my phone rang every 1.3 minutes, now I was lucky if it made a noise every 1.3 days. I had nothing to give them anymore. Even Caleb couldn't bear to be at my home in the country for longer than a night. The silence of the country created intrusive moments of reflection; we needed not to ponder on the lifestyle of our hedonistic culture. I hit my all-time low during my stay in the hospital for more tests, and having just one visitor—my trusted mother.

Staring at myself in a hospital gown, my hipbones sharp enough to poke a passerby, I acknowledged that I had brought this on myself. Desperate for approval, for love from anyone, I'd allowed myself to be burnt out. I'd given my soul to the devil, like Faustus, without even signing a contract.

I missed Dad and his advice, his warming affection. I wished I had a sibling to be of support for my mother who spent her nights pacing up and down the river. Most phone calls between myself and Caleb ended with him saying: "I have to work. You've just left me in London. You just up and left."

"But I'm ill?" I'd cry.

There was disconnection between him being sexual with me, yet being unable to tell me he loved me. Was I asking too much for a man to tie his actions to his words? Perhaps I was just paranoid due to the conditions I was under, but it was starting to seem evident that when I was on form, I was loved; when I was fragile, I was rejected. I was sick of fighting, sick of seeking meaning, sick of attempting to be something.

I often sat in the garden with no clear diagnosis, other than "an infection." Nothing could cure it other than a strong sedative painkiller. Truth was, I knew this called for something greater than a tiny pill. It called for a new perspective. I was playing the victim, feeling powerless in a time of my life when I thought I had taken control of the reins.

Why wasn't I able to adjust to this maddening world, to revel in the chaos like the others? Hounded by a deeper meaning to life, I read books on quantum physics, comprehending sentiments written by Dr. Emoto's *Hidden Messages in Water* for the first time. Too often we can't see the harm we do to others or ourselves unless we push someone physically against a glass wall and watch his tooth slide down the glass. Words have power; feelings have positive or negative effects on the body. Stress makes humans sick; joy can physically heal hearts. Light itself cannot be seen until it hits matter, a spectrum, and from it flies a thousand different colors. There is more than meets the eye.

This metaphysical fascination caused me to ponder constantly the desire to love and be loved in returned, why we were all like this. Wasn't that what everyone in advertising was trying to do? Wasn't that what they were trying to market to others? But their sense of worth was established in achievement, popularity, success, and money—all exhilarating virtues in their moments, but their gratification never had longevity. The awards would collect dust; the Bentleys dated; the popularity was conditional on a great idea; no one managed to have a stable relationship; such satisfaction could never be retained for long.

The recession had hit a year before, and as I watched a documentary on the economic decline, the Enron brothers marching out with their belongings in a box, I knew I was not alone in the search for a new identity. Something that didn't rely on mankind's materialism. My Louboutins hadn't been worn for months. My Vivienne Westwood was purchased in a state of panic, filling my void like milk through a sieve. Nothing worked. What was I really looking for? It wasn't just for a man who loved me; I wanted an identity within myself that I could bring to the table to anyone, not be reliant on another. In short, I hated codependency. After five months of ill health, members of my mother's church were the only ones who had consistently shown such kindness to me, bringing food, placing me on a prayer chain. As much as I wanted to push off the request to a God I didn't believe in, they meant well. I translated their prayers into "positive vibes" and kept watching episodes of *Keeping Up With The Kardashians*. Not only was I ill, I hated that I couldn't buy a Range Rover every Tuesday.

I called up the office to see the state of play with my health insurance, hoping that some money would contribute toward the medical tests that had surmounted to the worth of £2,000. Instead they told me their insurance wouldn't cover any of my hospital bills and found a way to make me redundant, which meant that they weren't contractually obligated to pay. I was sick, living with my mother, questioning my London friends' support, and now I was almost in a lawsuit, one that swiftly concluded after their lawyers realized the employer didn't even have a contract for me. My medical bill was paid, but I was now unemployed.

Within another month, Caleb, tired of the lowness of my health, the bad news I would boringly bring to every conversation on the phone, ended the relationship after eighteen months of us being together. I questioned if there were other women providing him the attention he obviously needed whilst I couldn't give it to him in London; he was shocked at such accusations.

Something within me always gave me these warnings.

This was the lowest time of my life since Pops had died. I was defeated. Dumbstruck. This hunger for the beyond was now hounding me. Episodic mentions of Christ, be it on television or in mother's prayer chain group, the peace of meditation described in Buddhism, and the beyond-the-self questions wouldn't leave me alone.

The most famous being on the planet for thoughts on love was, I hesitated to admit, Christ. In secret, I researched the reports of him outside of the Bible, descriptions of him from historical accounts, so untrusting of it since my religious days. He carried something that attracted people by the thousands. I thought about what he'd be like as my boss, as a brother, a father, my friend. I compared all my interactions with others in the last few years, everything from thrown paperwork, verbal abuse, and the girls who wished for my decline to Jesus' message about love. Jesus couldn't have been just some nice guy to be spoken about two thousand years later. He was both a lunatic and a liar, or He was God. And during this time, when an interviewer questioned the lead singer of *U2*, Bono, "Christ as Lord, isn't that a little farfetched?" Bono spurred a thought in me with his response, "I'm not joking here. The idea that the entire course of civilization for over half of the globe could have its fate changed and turned upside-down by a nutcase, for me, *that's* farfetched."

Was I researching about a man with the psychosis of a Charles Manson type, or was I investigating about the incarnation of God?

On a peaceful afternoon, I rested in the garden, content for the first time in a long time despite my circumstances telling me I should be trashing my bedroom in angst. Some overwhelming spontaneous presence came upon me; I was in some encounter that couldn't be seen by the eye, only felt by my soul—something I'd almost forgotten could happen. This awareness of the universe began to trigger emotional responses too deep and powerful for words. What if there *were* something? What if love actually made the world go around, and because mankind couldn't explain it, we reduced the word to our own comfortable understanding?

I looked to the sky and whispered, "I give up trying to give you up, God." The sense of not being alone strengthened, an indescribable peace increased, and I unfolded to the point of tears. "If You're there, whatever You are, if You are a father like this Christ talks of, I need to know You know the details of me. You count the strands of hair on my head, do You not? Show me one detail You see of me, God."

Silence.

I closed my eyes and exhaled. About to accuse myself of too much hope, I felt something on my nose. I opened my eyes, and a white butterfly, just like the one that had appeared from the flowers on my father's coffin five years before, flew off from the tip of my nose and circled around me. In a second, it disappeared.

I broke into a thousand whispered tears, while an inaudible voice kept saying: *I've been here all along.*

Such a small detail, such exuberant love. Unfazed by my arrogance, my bitterness, my need to perform—I was undone. I let go of the reins. I knew this wasn't logical, couldn't be explained on paper. But it was powerful, felt more *real* than Sparty's shoe to my head. I was too muddled to have invented this myself. It wasn't a crutch; I felt it quite the opposite actually. For the first time in years I stood with a greater stance, firmly on both legs. It took me out of myself; overwhelmed me with the proof that God had remembered my life, my tears, my joy. He had recorded it all. The butterfly had been a pivotal moment in my life, one in which I lost an earthly father. Was I now gaining a heavenly one?

He had never left me.

It was I who had left Him.

I began to listen to sermons differently; I soaked up scripture from a fatherly perspective. I dropped the victim mentality and reached out to Caleb, apologizing for the effect my illness had on me, on us. He came back to me just before my thirtieth birthday. I was ecstatic; winning the five billion dollar lottery would have been less exhilarating…or at least on par with it.

This understanding of an omnipotent father having sacrificed so much, having waited for so long for me to come home, began to invade my thinking. I was dreaming again, this time not for status or approval. What was it that I really wanted to do? I wrote a film script. I volunteered for a pregnancy crisis center, wanting to give a little back. I had dinner parties that didn't start with a Who's Who of introductions. I returned to advertising and moved back to London to live in a new flat. I tipped my cap when I saw Sparty, but I was happy to move on to smaller movers and shakers for a quieter, more meaningful life.

The Decadent Days

I felt more powerful now, ending unhealthy friendships that should have been cut years before. I began to have a fatherly perspective about daughters. I took better care of myself. Honesty and truth took an important role in my life. If a friend couldn't treasure honesty over pride, then we had very different core values.

But I still justified why it was okay to have sex; that Caleb and I loved each other, God was an all-loving, gracious God, and that the Bible's precepts were a little outdated—the contraceptive pill hadn't been invented way back then, and I was willing to have babies with him, so what was the problem? Because I had no conscience for conviction, little shame cropped up. Not only did I get rid of all the religion in me that meant nothing more than doctrinal law, I now found myself right in the middle of the grace-led movement. I'd swung to the other side. The problem was I mistook grace for being "anything goes and you'll still be loved" theology. I judged my actions by the surrounding culture, not on the guidance of a divine Father who was motivated by pure love.

Within months of my reunion with Caleb, I learned of his dishonesty and inappropriate relationships with women when I was in hospital, discoveries that changed my game plan. Friends at church asked why I wouldn't marry Caleb now after two years. I couldn't verbalize the answer. Deep down, I was bruised from the breakup, questioning if I'd ever feel protected by him in times of strife because surely difficult times were bound to happen again.

I'd been deceived many a time by Caleb. Sometimes there were questions of infidelity although nothing could be proven, and that was the problem: I never had firm answers. All this need to be loved by him was exhausting, and he equally didn't feel like he could do enough for me. I didn't care about making mistakes; I cared for honesty when they were made. I cared for communication when feelings needed to be expressed and understood. Both rarely occurred, and cracks began to show.

The inappropriate behavior with women was attention for his heart, yet negligence for mine. Sometimes I'd call the girls who had sent questionable texts to him, asking them for the truth, but they were about as helpful as unpicking a key lock with an anchovy.

It was here that I decided sex was too vulnerable. As awesome as it was, it didn't bring me life, just fear and emotional destruction when placed in negligent hands. I didn't value myself, and in the process, I was left to connect with a man who didn't have my best interest at heart. Sex did not create the beautiful love affairs we found in *Days of Thunder*; it just postponed our problems. The only wisdom I could receive was from the inaudible whisper from God, a whisper that came in my times of silence, that made me feel more alive than ever, more alert, more switched on, truly safe.

A new conviction unfolded the closer I got to God; I asked to try abstinence in my relationship with Caleb. It had nothing to do with the rules of the Bible even though I now wondered if God had created sexual pleasure only for those who were willing to be fully committed to another, not like this partial commitment I was facing. It had everything to do with wanting to build a healthy foundation of patience, kindness, and emotional respect. In Caleb's defense, all of these meandering mistakes were part of the years of us growing up, discovering what compromise meant. Most of what he learned in our relationship he never carried out again, and neither did I. And we did build our love for a time. We were still the greatest of friends.

On my thirtieth birthday, he gave me an eternity ring at my father's grave, vowing to take care of me, to protect me, to value my heart. It was a tearful moment for both of us. The diamond ring glistened over my father's epitaph. It was thoughtful, beautiful. Filled with forgiveness.

The Decadent Days

In this same year, Marina Abramovic, the artist I couldn't comprehend, exhibited an installation at the MOMA, called "The Artist Is Present." A collation of her life's work was to be shown for three months, whilst Marina herself sat on a wooden chair in an exuberant red gown for seven and a half hours a day. Opposite her was an empty chair, one in which members of the public could sit in and stare at her. The creative directors of MOMA were concerned for her health, but she was determined to see the show through. Thousands queued, sleeping overnight on the streets to have just a few minutes to engage with her. No talking, no touching, no unusual activity (although some did try). So many fell into tears; some found euphoria. A few even got tattoos of their ticket numbers since the interaction left them stunned and breathless. The experience was being compared to an encounter with Christ.

And oh how ironic I found it all. People waiting for hours to have an encounter that included no physical touching or verbal understanding. People hungered for these moments more than sexual connections. The only man Marina reached out to touch in this artistic stare-down was her former lover for over a decade, with whom she had created many famous performance pieces. As Ulay sat down in the facing chair, she opened her eyes with silent tears. There was tension in the air. What would happen between the lovers who used to slap each other in the face on film, the ones who, owning nothing but a truck, travelled Europe together? After three minutes, which was a long time for this exhibit, she lifted her hands up and toward him, a form of surrender, a sign of peace. He smiled, reached to hold her hands, while the standing audience that layered floor upon floor of the MOMA, flooded the place with applause and cheers.

No one had sex. No one even kissed. All was forgiven. Journalists began reporting; cameras flashed like the paparazzi.

This sensitivity to emotion, to kindness made me speak up when observing this interaction take place: "If this is what it is like with Marina, just a Serbian artist with a temporary installation at MOMA, what would that interaction have been like with Christ?"

I thought of the accounts, the historical reports I'd been reading outside of the Bible. The moments where people fell to the floor, the thousands who wanted to hear His wisdom on forgiveness, morality, creation, Heaven. The ones who carried their loved ones on stretchers in the belief that He could turn their lives around and heal them.

"Christ? The Son of God? It's hardly plausible is it?" My friend standing next to me retorted.

"Why?" I asked. "I think He's a masterpiece. A very plausible masterpiece."

CHAPTER 9

Make Love, Not Porn

Returning back to the rocky road of abstinence in my late twenties, I stumbled upon a new form of stimulation, one that I bizarrely believed caused less harm—porn. When GQ magazine released the article "10 Reasons Why You Should Quit Watching Porn," everyone rubbed their eyes and re-read the title. Surely GQ would support an article titled, "10 Reasons Why You Should Dump Your Girlfriend and Click Online"? Isn't it mandatory for them to print pictures of the sexiest women wearing nothing but a man's shirt with hints of skin on every other page? [2]

I knew this had become a cultural issue when such a magazine controversially opposed that which society had accepted into the "tolerate" bracket. I knew we were going too far when David Cameron restricted pornographic websites from the British nation.

Once I began to abstain from sex in my relationship with Caleb, I still continued to date him; he was very understanding (I guess he could have left), and I still desired him in every way. I turned to pornography to stave off any temptation, thinking I was helping matters. I appeased my needs and even sent Caleb the links to check it out himself, hoping he wouldn't feel neglected.

And yet, soft pornography wasn't new to my world. I remember walking through some of the floors when working in publishing, noting that the lad's mags, the motorcycling magazines, and the automotive titles all used the female body as a direct form of sensational stimulation. Such magazine titles were in full revenue swing, with big budgets and big female "assets" littering the walls from floor to ceiling. Women weren't just being objectified—their bodies became our wallpaper. The men in the office didn't look at me for my personality, they were valuing my credentials–and we're not talking about my resume. When we photographed models for many of our best-selling platforms, they were brought in through the back door and covered with large coats and plastic platforms. As a girl would pass me, I'd give her the token "we all know you're about to get naked" look. And yet, she didn't hold her head in pride as I passed her in a pair of jeans, notebook and pen in hand. She held nothing but the rim of her coat, pulling the opening a little closer together as if she were cold. There was a sense of shame because we all knew she did it for the money and it wasn't even that much. I wanted to rescue her from the studio filled with men, lenses, and body oil. I held the stare for longer sometimes, so she wouldn't feel alone. But she'd soon disconnect, focusing back on the room, allowing the door to shut behind her.

I remembered those exchanges vividly, my heart going out to the girls, and yet here I was endorsing the entire industry. I didn't need to buy a wrapped magazine from the top shelf or borrow my mate's DVDs. I worked with biker boys and car testers who had an ample supply.

Slowly soft pornography needed to be a little more graphic, a little more rough around the edges, less of a story, less chit chat, more action, more people involved. Before I knew it, only after a few months—long enough to claim it as a habit—I was watching stuff you'd scream at should you stumble upon it in the flesh. When it came to a girl being used by one too many men, I caught myself speaking out, "WHAT IN HELL'S NAME AM I WATCHING?"

Friends and I believed the lie that porn didn't harm anyone, that it was just a little sexual kick, nothing to worry about. That was, until I looked my man in the eyes and realized something had changed. I was no longer rendered breathless by a look from him, nor was he with me. Sensitivity had vanished in our relationship, so respect followed suit. We were stimulated by different, more graphic images; what the Internet had to offer became more powerful than our own connection. If evil in the world came down to disassociating ourselves with love and kindness, then surely there was no better way to describe pornography, which filled our brains with lustful images and animalistic excitement before boys and girls even met anyone with whom to fall in love, to serve, to cherish.

My desensitization was due to what neuroscientists call "opening new neural pathways," inducing an orgasm from visually pornographic images. This Pavlovian approach was self-serving, the sexual images pervasive. It did not encourage love but, instead, dissolved it. In short, the approach made me begin to believe, "I don't care if your sexual parts belong to you any more, or that they do anything for you; I care about what it does for me."

Married couples often sought help from therapists when the screen gained more attention than the spouse. When the puppet master of pornography dictated the sex drive, we lost control of what inspired us. Those of us who succumbed believed we didn't need intimacy when we had porn, but the irony was that porn made me feel lonelier than ever before.

In tests, a porn addict's brain scan showed brain waves no different to that of a crack addict, according to Cambridge students. And with almost fifty percent of porn users never having had sex in the real world, with real people, then Houston, we definitely had a problem. We had already destroyed any chance of real intimacy with a potential marriage partner.

I've never taken drugs thanks in part to Pete's overdose and resulting suicide in high school, but mainly because I knew it would open me up to an experience that I'd want to return to again and again. Because I wasn't ignorant as to how drugs made people feel, there was no temptation and no downward spiral into the worse states of drug use. I still had a fabulous time without the help of drugs since I knew nothing else. Yet I didn't realize that porn could have the same addictive effect. Everywhere I turned, more people were speaking out against it. Allison Pearson, a columnist for the *The Daily Telegraph*, began writing articles about the issue, claiming, "Pornography is warping the behavior of boys against girls." [3]

I'd sit in a pub listening to the filth coming out of fourteen-year-olds, and my word, how I missed innocence. While we weren't squeaky clean ourselves back then, surely we were able to have some decent repartee, conversations filled with original thought and a form of humor that didn't degrade the opposite sex.

But were these arguments any different than those that suggested violent video games desensitized our youth, even leading some young kids to bring guns to school? Not all kids illegally obtained an AK-47 and annihilated their classmates; perhaps not all porn users were becoming hazardous to society, right? So we stayed silent about pornography, keeping it an individual pastime, thinking it caused no injury. But I was already seeing a change in my own intimacy with my boyfriend. I also became suspicious that any man could be exclusive; all they wanted was sex, so we as women performed, becoming more provocative in social interaction and risqué selfies.

Older male friends, ones in their late-forties, were a step ahead of me, with nothing left to hold onto but the remaining ashes of burnt porn, fed up of finding themselves in continuous one night stands or fortnightly love affairs, despairing for a real connection. Others denied all knowledge of being involved with porn at all. Even with a ten-year age gap, there was still the subtle embarrassment of needing "material."

"I'm not looking at women like I used to," my friend Tex honestly admitted. "I'd like a little stimulation to the brain as well as my eyes."

"How long have you been using porn for?" I asked, delving into a packet of crisps. It was so mild to me now, even the topic was as nonchalant as the weather forecast.

"WHAT?! That's an absurd suggestion! What has this got anything to do with porn? Do you have such a little opinion that you'd think I've some sordid addiction to pornography? I can have real-life sex, thank you very much. I mean to *assume*—"

"Tex—there's some on that shelf behind your head." I smiled.

"WHO PUT THAT THERE?!"

"You did. I categorized your videos by genre last time I visited."

"You must have been high."

"Really? Are we going to continue down this road of denial?"

"Yes. Yes, we are. Okay. No," Tex folded.

Even if there weren't a back catalogue of poorly cinematographed porn on his bookshelf, I could spot regular users a mile away. They switched off in conversation pretty quickly; they listened to my thoughts with the attention span of a Dachshund puppy, and I like to think I have some pretty stimulating badinage. There was less patience, and after a few drinks, they needed some physical interaction with a woman. If a male friend and I were dining alone, I would end up being the target. In short, people got bored because they were spending a lot of time being spoon-fed sexual eroticism whenever they wanted it.

The idea that porn was harmless was instantly invalidated by human rights organizations. Sex-trafficking abolishment charities were beginning to see a direct relationship between pornography and trafficking. As a friend of mine who leads a non-profit agency against trafficking described: "There is a growing body of research that looks at the correlation between violent pornography and the increase in violent male sexual behavior. Does that mean that all men who watch violent pornography will rape a woman? Of course not. However, most men who rape attest that they are users of violent pornography."

I heard another story of a highly respected teacher who delved into soft porn during a rough patch in his marriage. He viewed it as "light fun" to experience a form of freedom from the powerlessness he was feeling. Two years later he found himself in prison, having been caught with child pornography, something he never anticipated.

We may not have felt it was harmful in our private moments, but the residual effects of continuous graphic images were creating a brand new world filled with self-gratification and dehumanization. I was becoming increasingly aware that it was no different from me puffing on a Marlboro and telling some fifteen-year-old, "You don't wanna start, Kid. It'll only cost you money—then your life. Now go and play Tiddlywinks." It wasn't worth the addiction.

Around the same time as my abstinence from sex and this new addition to the list (porn), I began volunteering at a pregnancy crisis center on my days off. A few months of training allowed me to work with some young girls, panicked they were pregnant or panicked that they weren't. Learning the pregnancy outcome was almost a side dish to the learning I gained in relationships, identity, and sexuality. As the tears of a fourteen-year-old girl who didn't want to be pregnant began to flow when her test showed positive, she opened up to me about her boyfriend. How he didn't want to use a condom, how rough and animal-like he was in the bedroom, how he hadn't returned her calls since she first thought she might be pregnant. She had sacrificed herself to appease him, and along the way, picked up an addiction to porn in the hope she could learn new things. Yet all it did was tear her insides apart and create a new life she wasn't ready for.

The more I began counseling friends and clients in the crisis center, the more damage I saw from the modern-day world of an overly sexualized culture. As long as porn was the main go-to for a man (or woman) to feel powerful, our relationships would be damaged. And this was the irony: The use of such content was really only there for when we were feeling lonely, sexually frustrated, or unknown. It was never deemed a productive use of my time. I was struggling to keep a boyfriend exclusive to me in his conduct with other women. With all my insecurity, occasionally strengthened by the attention of women, the last thing I needed was for him to be fed graphic images of naked women on a consistent basis.

Some marriages I knew about were willing to work through the porn addiction, while some gave up, finalizing their divorce with the addicted partners seeking for someone that could sexually fulfill them, which was a futile dream that often only led to more isolation, depression, and loneliness. Shame would begin to spread like cancer after the climax was done, and once the laptop was closed, the eyes glared around an empty bedroom. Mates would have pangs of guilt in the daytime, sometimes throwing away all their mags, DVDs, cyber links, registering to accountability programs for help, hoping to reboot their memories to a simpler time. But nothing could erase the brain. There was no delete button for memories, just the hope it would fade.

Broadcaster Louis Theroux explored the porn industry in one documentary, revisiting years later to find that some stars had committed suicide or turned to prostitution to make ends meet, and one had made more adult films to cope with the death of a baby. People weren't working in the porn industry when they were happy; they turned to it when they were misunderstood, in pain, out of options. But it wasn't the end. I saw wives or husbands get rid of the magazines, come out of sex chat rooms, exit fetish clubs, and turn down offers of high class orgies disguised as "stately home masquerade parties." These were the ones who told me that their sexual functions actually improved. Relationships found connection again. Some even felt fully loved for the very first time. As long as the stuff wasn't revisited again. [4]

Still, women who became porn artists signed on the dotted line. They agreed to partake in the industry, so to say that we dehumanized them didn't feel right—for the most part, it was their choice. But then there were the side businesses that gained income from the residue of the sex industry, and this was where I saw a whole other perspective.

In my early thirties, years past my short-lived porn addiction, my missionary work began to take full flow. As part of my ministry school training in California, I traveled to the Philippines to counsel girls in high trauma. When I came face-to-face with young victims of sex trafficking, my view on porn changed even more. I saw that not only was it a relationship buster, demonic in its aim, but porn was instigating the things done to the girls. Economic decline and international transportation were merely helpful additions that made Southeast Asia one of the most plagued parts of the developing world for sex trafficking. My friend who rescues girls and women out of trafficking shared this with me:

Make Love, Not Porn

I remember walking down the street in Pattaya, Thailand and seeing a beautiful, young, scantily clad Thai girl walking down the street with a very unattractive, almost gruesome-looking Western man. Pattaya is the sex tourism capital of the world, and many tourists go to Pattaya to solicit sex from the girls forced to work in the bars and brothels. The young Thai girl was doing what most women would have a difficult time doing… she was hanging on the man's every word, gaze locked, laughing and giggling at his every movement. What struck me from this encounter was that for probably around $4, this troubled man had done the unthinkable—he had won the undeserved gaze of a beautiful young girl for whom he had not paid the price of relationship, marriage, or even self-development. His $4 in Thailand had bought him the same thing that $4 buys a man watching porn…for that brief moment he felt powerful.

When I travelled there, I also met girls who were being raped night after night for $4. Just $4. Heartbreak got the better of me as I watched Western men in Manila airport on their phones, booking their next destinations—the bars. You think pedophiles are a rarity, but there were thousands of them there to get their live sex kicks thanks to the cunning inspiration of bad story lines, baby oil, and home video cameras.

Friends from around the globe emailed me stories, the worst case being when a friend had managed to record a phone conversation with another man who was the negotiator seeking to kidnap children from Russian orphanages and sell them to traffickers. As my friend witnessed and trialed for the UN, he saw pictures of eighteen-month-old bodies that had died from internal bleeding due to rape. All culprits had watched porn. There is no chicken and egg question here, whether porn instigated the events or whether porn was viewed to satiate their desires. It *encouraged* this evil behavior, the torture, the nauseating crimes.

When dealing with the pimps themselves, I didn't understand just how evil they could be. One of my girlfriends, Katie, who found the insurmountable love of Christ in jail after being involved in sex-trafficking rings for a few years, told me that when one guy proposed the idea of her working for him, he sat her down at a table and warned: "You do know I'm the devil, don't you?"

Pimps had no problem throwing girls onto the streets with the ugliest of STDs, deeming them "no use" by the time they were fifteen. They had no conscience. They had no desire for anything other than to rip the souls from the women and sell their bodies like meat.

My friend talked about the effects that porn had on her clients, making them less human, more monster. The more they built porn into their daily lives, the more they had no problem with calling her number.

Just because we watched a free preview online that lasted no longer than five minutes—it didn't mean our conscience was clean of crime. One click on one of these websites and, just like the ignorant pot users who bought a tiny amount of dope to get a better high once in a while, porn addicts involved themselves in the chain of events that allowed a business to exceed trillions in revenue, costing our governments millions to eradicate its side effects—murder, rape, kidnapping, sexual diseases, death. It was time for me to wake up and come out from the duvet of denial I had been hiding under.

Knowing how objectifying it was, I began experiencing a toxic response to seeing pornographic images. I couldn't watch it without shame anymore. I was convicted, and I understood why. Conviction was a time for celebration; after all, it meant I was learning something. True conviction, unlike shame and condemnation, rarely comes from the wrong perspective and is usually a sign of wisdom and maturity. And that's why I celebrated. I was about to change, and for the better. Distorted views of sex could make me feel powerful in the moment, but just as the antonym of the word *power* is *impotence*, so, too, would the exploration into that world make me finally impotent to find freedom and true gratification. Porn was a trap behind closed doors that literally brainwashed humans into believing they were getting their kicks from strangers having sex. Evil cloaked sex in lust, hoping we would mistake it for freedom.

Many of us fell for porn in a bad patch when the soul was dehydrated. We drank and drank, and yet we were still thirsty, and that thirst was never quenched. Those who had fallen into the addictive grip had been poisoned with more lies, detaching the physical from the emotional. However powerful I believed porn was, it was up to me if I wanted to sign up. But in the darkness of the night and the freshness of a new morning, I considered the pinnacle question that began to lead many of my decisions: "Did it bring me life? Or would it bring a slow death? To the world? To my lover? Most importantly, to myself?"

Fed up, I rejected porn like I did contaminated food and sought for a new beginning. The more reality bit me, the more I questioned myself. Like many of my male friends who had found themselves marinating in pornographic paraphernalia, the sense of conviction, of objectification, of "this is stupid," of "you're alone, trying to get false intimacy from a computer screen" crushed any desire for the stuff. I still wasn't fulfilled, I wasn't connected to a person, and my disconnection with Caleb was being stretched further still.

Turning thirty is always a maze to manage, but in this particular instance, I had quite a wild past to look back upon. And I didn't feel good. I didn't feel good at all. Conviction had turned itself into shame, and even though I believed I had finally escaped the entrapment of sordid pleasures and empty kisses, the greatest toxin was knocking on my door, one that kept some from never being free, no matter how well we were behaving.

CHAPTER 10

The "F" Word

After another two years of sharing a joint business and a community of friends and family, Caleb and I still had not made it to the altar. As my spirituality deepened, his faith took a ride up a different hill, often describing the difference between our beliefs to others: "I compartmentalize my belief in God, whereas Carrie would give up everything for Him."

He was right. I'd never understand why I would believe in God at all if I couldn't make Him my everything. Transformation and restoration don't happen one day a week; they happen every waking second of the day. I didn't want my faith to be an afterthought. To expect Caleb to make God his everything would have been quite a stretch, especially since he wouldn't even give up his luxury apartment and move five minutes away so we could both afford to live together. He cared for luxury and location; I'd learned that I would be happy living in a wigwam if it meant being with the one I loved.

And so, the next chapter of our lives together is titled in remembrance of his female cohort. He told me she was a friend of a friend. Someone he'd met only a few times. He told me the finger puppets she'd sent for his nephew's Christmas present meant nothing. Just a friendly gesture. They had become friends on Facebook the day before his birthday. Her profile usually involved her standing on her head, as if she were a descendant of Mr. Contortionist himself. Her name was Fiona Faulkner and a few days after Caleb added her to Facebook, he finished with me.

I had trusted his sentiments. After all, we had been in a serious relationship for quite a while now, and he was only one of the three sexual partners I'd ever had. Why shouldn't I trust him? Why shouldn't I believe that this girl, whom he had mentioned a couple of times over dinner, was nothing to him? He flicked it away like an irritating fly, but I wasn't ready to swat it just yet. It took four months and an episode of *The Graham Norton Show* on BBC iPlayer to learn the reality of my world. I was watching the show on my man's computer when he had fallen asleep. I closed the window on the laptop and found *fifty* emails all addressed to the girl who "meant as much as a blue bottle." Curiosity killed this kitten as I fumbled through each email, shaking, wishing I could suspend my belief, but it was hung out to dry, quite like the trust I now had for the boyfriend fast asleep.

Full of flirtatiousness and plans to call or email when the "other halves" were not around, these conversations also betrayed something more serious: a night my boyfriend described as a moment that "should never have happened." He asked to just be friends with her, stating that he wanted to focus on his relationship with me.

Of all the things I can tolerate, lying isn't one of them. It was unbearable to find out I had less knowledge of my own relationship than some girl who loved to run events and read a Shel Silverstein book. Let's hope to the Lord she doesn't read this one.

They bantered between each other like my heart didn't exist. They communicated with empty nothings, ramping up the flirt before it hit the fan somewhere between a Wednesday night and a Thursday morning. It wasn't clear in the emails, but Caleb obviously felt too guilty to continue.

I closed the laptop. I couldn't find my bag and so turned the light on, much to my frustration. I wanted to leave without him knowing.

He awoke like a mole finding light after a good dig in a long tunnel. "What are you doing?"

I looked at him, lost in my own hurt and confusion, perturbed as to why he couldn't stick to my number one need in our relationship, which was: No matter what mistake you make, tell me so that I can still always trust you to be honest. I took a breath, picked up my case, straightened my jacket, and took a look around the room one last time.

"I have two words for you: Fiona Faulkner." I stood there long enough to see his reaction, to watch conviction hit him like a bulldozer, before I walked through the front door, turning before I left to watch him puke by the side of the bed in guilt.

By the time I got in a cab, London felt so vast and empty. I was on autopilot and full of rage. I dared not talk to the cab driver. I called the only friend I knew who would be up at 3:00 a.m. on a Saturday night. In true friendship form, Charlie arrived on my door in Notting Hill, knowing it must have been an emergency with a tub of Ben and Jerry's (for her), a pack of cigarettes (for me), and a frown on her face. This wasn't the first time my boyfriend had lied, and I was almost certain it wouldn't be the last time either if I stayed with him.

He called in the morning, devastated, yet relieved he didn't have to feel guilty anymore. Marvelous for him, sucky for me. No amount of begging, kneeling on the floor with tears in the eyes was convincing, although witnessing him squirm did, in all honesty, help. Wanting sweet revenge is pretty natural when you've been sucker punched with fifty plus emails to a girl whom your boyfriend "doesn't really know." Perhaps he didn't know enough about her in order to state that he knew her? Perhaps we don't really know anyone until we learn if the other's had his or her tonsils out, and quite frankly, with the suggestive actions taking place, I think he probably knew at least that much about her.

I took a month away from him before, like the devalued human I felt I was, I took him back. Wishful that we could move on, hopeful that I could mend my broken heart. I began to understand why women stayed in abusive relationships: It seemed that the man who created your downfall was the only one who could build it back up again. It was codependency on overdrive.

Even though I continued to date him, I never really did forgive him. He welded himself to me, cut all ties with any female who had a connection with Fiona, and began to speak up if a girl showed interest. Problem was, he already showed me he had the capacity to lie, and so I rested somewhere in purgatory, otherwise known as unforgiveness. I tried to forgive, tried to rewrite the past, tried to pretend at least that all was well. But inwardly, I was suffocating in denial.

The haunting of this lack of closure never allowed me to move forward. I'd pray, I'd remind myself of all the things I'd done wrong, but the feeling still remained. Forgiveness is similar to judo. It is an art form that must be motivated by a fighting spirit, with no choice but to hold on throughout the battle until we've won. Forgiveness fights against its opponent bitterness, throwing it down to the mat to achieve victory. At the same time, we fight against ourselves, unsure how to react to the heinous thoughts and crimes of others who have hurt us. And yet I had to learn to react using the same approach as judo, which means "the gentle way."

Absolution could not be given by retaliating because, as my late Grandma James would tell me, "revenge has two graves." Yet my mind created wild imaginings of the justice I could seek within the confusion of my pain. I wanted everyone to join in, backing up how gruesome the other person's soul was to cheat, lie, steal, kill, and dishonor. Character defamation had never been so tempting, along with those angry subliminal social online statuses. But that ugliness could begin to cultivate my own beastly disfiguration. I did have some dignity, or perhaps it was pride. My soul was not what it was before the event. I was barely able to recognize my own eyes in the mirror.

Years could pass by, and I could still be carrying this hardened shell filled with poison, not even noticing the change in myself. For the emotion of bitterness had become my guarded friend, ensuring I never got vulnerable so no one could hurt me again. Forgiveness was and is still the greatest misconception in Christianity, which has given us our PR image of Scrooge rather than Saint Nicholas. Communities divide, intimacy suffocates amongst the Church family, and before we know it, no one is allowed to make a mistake. Oh, people claim they have forgiven each other, but we need only see their interaction with a past loved one to know they've not forgiven them any more than Scar forgave Mufasa in *The Lion King*. They still harbor feelings of antipathy although outwardly "they've forgiven." And of course they have—the Bible told them to.

Hearts as gelid as frosted snow form in the very people who once loved others beautifully. If only they'd drop the grudge. It might have been years since a person's father abused them or mother left them, yet a person's whole life could be constructed to avoid hurt or pain, letting no one in. I was beginning to realize why some men and women couldn't follow through with falling in love. I just had to ask people about their relationships with their parents. Fearful of gauging emotions that placed them on a vulnerable platform, it was much easier to list a few things wrong with each (wo)man they initially liked than face the real demon within: the resentment of their own parent(s). Had I done the same? Had I transferred some unforgiveness with my father into a similar man, and now I couldn't trust any male?

Life had become a constant hopscotch of living in reaction to pasts that should have been shown grace a long time ago. It was so easy to forgive someone who had hurt me when he knelt at my front door with tears running down the guitar he used to serenade me with, begging for an acknowledgement that he didn't really mean it. It was so much harder to forgive when memories of those emails would resurface.

However, forgiveness really was a self-repair program that was required in order for me to avoid depression, low self-esteem, and the toxin caused by bitterness. This wasn't fluff, this was basic biology. I wouldn't dream of suggesting that all cancer is caused by bitterness, but more than once I have seen people be healed from cancer, their tumors literally disappearing, after acknowledging that they had been unforgiving toward someone who had caused them severe pain. Once they let it go and forgave, they were healed. Medical reports then later confirmed this, confusing the doctors and astounding the patients.

"But there are just some things we can't forgive," is the classic go-to response that I heard in counseling sessions and or even conversations in coffee shops.

Forgiveness is not the notion that you have to open the door to your heart the moment a person whispers, "Sorry." It doesn't condone abuse in any form. It doesn't mean we ignore the hurt someone caused. For me, forgiveness wasn't a way to benefit the person I was forgiving, but to benefit myself. Just like ice couldn't stay the same in Saharan temperatures, I decided that unforgiveness could not survive when I allowed the warmth of self-love to alter my heart. When I really loved who I was on my not-so-great days, I started to find it incredibly hard to harbor ill feelings toward those who hurt me. It was becoming easier to jab pride in the collarbone and humble myself because I knew that I, too, had hurt others. I knew that I didn't deserve a man's poor treatment, but I was strong enough to know that his hurt was not about me personally, but his own brokenness.

So how do I forgive? I had to allow for a time to process, to be angry, to cry it out. Forgiveness didn't mean I couldn't be upset, that I couldn't allow my pain to have a voice; after all, stifling the hurt was one of the main reasons why people couldn't find forgiveness and therefore compassion. So with a spoonful of sharing the mess in the secret place, private dialogues with God, a punch or two of a pillow, and finally, a grasping of someone else's life to attempt to understand (not condone) the brokenness that led him to hurting me, I could start seeing things clearly. I addressed the drinking days of my father, the selfish ploys of past boyfriends, and the lack of value I had for myself. It turned out, the greatest forgiveness I needed to extend was for little ole' me.

It was only here that forgiveness truly began. Then I could finally see my father as someone unloved by his own father; I saw my boyfriends, all clueless on how to love when they didn't know how to receive love themselves; I saw myself, doing the best I could with the fear of loss following my feet. Walking through pain was the only way to forgiveness. I *had* to face it. I needed to work through the torment to come through the other side, all the while being gentle on myself. I let myself be as messy as I wanted to be in front of my ever constant, ever faithful divine Essence, the One I had discovered was a greater Father than any earthly male. I became my whole self again, and I fully accepted who I was. It was from that internal place that I could rationally respond to someone whose thoughtlessness could have broken me for more than a day. It was from there that I could smile at them and shake them by the hand. If they were unhealthy folk, I didn't waste my focus on their opinion of me. It was from there that I could form a new boundary with someone, knowing that we have very different core values.

I've had seasons in which I've struggled to forgive, but the joy I've found in my faith was the realization that I could turn to the very God who forgave me before I was even imagined in His mind. Not because God was some sort of crutch to me, some form of codependency in itself, but because the humanified version of God had not sought revenge against those who desired to kill him. I had Christ as a reference, the man who exemplified it.

Most people of faith understand the theology behind the need for forgiveness. Christ didn't suffer the world's most intolerable capital punishment just for me to miss the point of perfect love, poisoning myself with hatred toward someone who stole my Nokia twelve years ago. Or even toward the one who trafficked someone's body, like the girls I've counseled. Most righteous believers know *why* they should forgive, but they are still faced with defensive reactions and distrust toward people after they've been affected by one of the three Ds: divorce, death, or disarming of the soul. When I'd finally worked through the pain, the compassion came a little easier, and I became fed up with being fed up. This process was impossible as long as there was pride, fear of emotion, or an unwillingness to become vulnerable. Only emotional leverage could make me change perspective.

Ten years ago I walked into an art exhibition purely by accident. It showed a bunch of photographs of unrecognizable faces, all representing true-life accounts. The visuals were about as entertaining as my own cooking (that's not a good thing), but the stories attached to them changed my mind. From Desmond Tutu to a mother who had lost her son after a drunk driver killed him, all were based on individual journeys to forgiveness. Genuine "heart-meant" forgiveness. Two married missionaries had been taken hostage by Chechnyan soldiers for fourteen torturous months. The wife was taken into another room and repeatedly raped by one of the guards while the husband was handcuffed to heated pipes. It's a level of suffering that doesn't happen to many of us. As she contracted herpes, terrified of raising an alarm in case the other soldiers developed the idea of gang rape, the couple faced more pain than most could survive. Within her mind, the wife refused to let the rapist damage her inner peace, knowing her body was not all of her. The husband repeatedly fantasized about murdering the soldier but instead chose to react with prayer for him. On release, despite the joy and the freedom from captivity, the wife collapsed. They both needed some time apart to heal and go through their own emotional recovery. Once they both admitted the pain, through weakness and vulnerability, they were slowly able to heal, acknowledging the guards were taught to be cruel. There was an understanding, but not atonement. They weren't planning to reconcile with their captors, but still they found freedom in forgiveness. No one wins when we get revenge. I've never seen vendettas mend anyone's soul, just break it more. I've never seen love come from those who don't believe in forgiveness.

As I read and heard more stories of forgiveness, I was becoming more inspired by story upon story of the fruit of mercy, overwhelmed by the supreme strength of grace: There was Yvonne Stern, who in 2010 forgave her husband for his affair along with the mistress who tried to get rid of her by hiring a hit man. Then there was Gordon Wilson's forgiveness toward the IRA bombers who killed his daughter, which rocked the peace movement for Northern Ireland. Even Ruby Bridges, a six-year-old black girl, who in 1960 prayed along the corridors of an all-white school in New Orleans while others shouted, threw things, and threatened poisoning. She set the course for the beginning of integrated schools. [5]

These days I never underestimate the power of the pardon. People only ever remember the names of those who refuse to hide behind the pain and forgive those who caused the atrocities they suffered. No one remembered the names of many other relatives of the IRA victims, just Gordon Wilson, because his grace startled souls. The freedom of forgiveness creates a domino effect of love, which has, in some cases, changed the course of history forever.

A year after renewing my relationship with Caleb—the one where I had decided to abstain from sex, picked up porn, put down porn, and decided to find myself again post Fiona Faulkner—I began to see a little more clearly. My thoughts were filtering through the shame and not holding onto bitterness. My own strength had grown to levels that made me love friends, family, and everyone in general far better. I could discern if a man was too controlling; I could discern if a man was loving me for his own selfish benefit rather than considering my heart; I could forgive, and forgive quickly. I had no idea how close it was to becoming a habit.

Though we still loved each other, I knew the time had come for Caleb and I to break up—no small feat after five years together. As I walked in these new epiphanies, I still had days where I questioned if I had made the right decision; we had come through so much, despite the hurdles. True to form, it was these days when God would plant another seed. One such morning, I asked for my non-fat latte in an Oregon coffee shop, taking a mini-break from life in Northern California. In front of me was a woman, twitching, as if she knew me, though I'd never seen her in my life. She was American, with long hair and blue eyes, as fidgety as a three-year-old needing to pee.

"I'm sorry," she said, turning to me. "You don't know me, and you must forgive me for the intrusion here. I'm not even sure if this is accurate."

"Okay?" I responded with an ounce of suspicion.

"I feel like you made a decision within the last year, and that decision has directly affected the happiness of your future children. So on their behalf, the children who are yet to be born, thank you."

I stared at her for a minute, questioning if she had read my journal or hacked my email account. But no. "Are you a Christian?" I asked.

"Yes," she said.

"Then you are correct. And you heard from our Father correctly. Thank you." I shook her by the hand.

I excused myself from the line and walked to a park nearby. I sat on a bench, looked up to the sky as tears rolled down my face.

All was forgiven. I was forgiven. He was forgiven.

My power was not in the withholding of mercy; my power only came to fruition in my pardon. In the process, I saw my own reflection in all its clarity and in all its beauty.

No one now could hold the very peace I was given from the beginning of time. Impunity was never a battle of the egos, nor a battle of scorecards.

The goal of forgiveness was always to love myself first.

CHAPTER 11

Poison in a Pint

"I waited. For that day. I was patient to wear white. I was deliriously excited about all this sex I was finally going to have. But I found myself unclothed and completely ashamed. I didn't enjoy it. I didn't want to do it. I was compliant to keep him happy. But my God, Carrie. The shame. The shame. The shame." My girl, Patsy, put her gin and tonic down.

I was on break from ministry school, visiting friends back home in England like Patsy, who had recently married. Both of us in our early thirties, we were discussing the ups-and-downs of the past decade, the conversation turning to her unexpected disappointment. "I'm sorry." I frowned. "I didn't know it was Burlesque night. This is beyond the pale choice of location, considering our topic."

Petal, a dancer, was parading on the tiny cabaret stage as a backdrop to our conversation in an East London bar. Patsy looked over at Petal who was splashing around in a giant martini glass, wearing blue sapphires as a costume. There were two other people in the entire place: Matt the bartender and Gary, a guy who spent all of his welfare money most evenings in this establishment and therefore paid Matt's wage. Gary wasn't even watching the performance; instead he chose to complete *The Times* crossword puzzle, accompanied by half a pint of shandy.

"Perhaps she could give me some one-on-one coaching, then all would be well," Pats said sarcastically. She was about to celebrate her first year of marriage, betrothed to the one she loved but couldn't open up to sexually. She had no idea that when they transferred their love to the bedroom for the first time, she would experience shame, confusion, and fragility more than ever before. She loved her man, she hated the sex—a frustration we couldn't have imagined before, when sex was something we dreamed about having once we found covenant.

"Here am I," I said over Petal's intriguing recital of *Happy Birthday, Mr. President.* "Down three sexual relationships that never made it to the altar, the words 'former porn addict' added to my resume, and most of my reformed celibate mates are former prostitutes or gang members with stories that would make Quentin Tarantino blush, yet I've got this bizarre sense that you carry more shame than we do? The girl with the squeaky clean past is punishing herself for no reason at all."

"I know. I don't know where it's come from." Pats swirled her gin around with her straw.

"Did you allow yourself to have feelings—even though you needed to manage them—before you were married? Or did you gulp those desires down like a tube of Pringles because you thought they were evil?"

"I guess I was proud of never taking a step out of place. I was proud that I was in complete control."

"Who invented the orgasm?" I was now on a mission to find the real answers by asking questions like a contestant on *Jeopardy*.

"A mignon of the anti-Christ?" She was being quite serious.

"This might be wherein the problem lies..." I remarked.

Pats looked even more lost.

"I've no idea which random book you've been reading, but it ain't the Bible, sweetheart. Sex was meant to be pleasurable, no? We could have procreated like an anglerfish," I added.

"What?" She seemed overwhelmed. I think I had lost Pat's train of thought somewhere after the word *orgasm*.

"They're probably the ugliest fish you've ever seen," I explained. "The males are born without a digestive system, so in order to survive, they must immediately attach themselves to a female after hatching. They do this by biting her to release an enzyme that fuses the two together. Forever. Eventually, the male's brain, eyes, and organs dissolve until he turns into a small lump, with only his sexual organs remaining. When the female is ready to reproduce, sperm is released from the 'lump' and the female is fertilized."

"Is this supposed to make me feel like making love to my husband?" Pats asked.

I needed to change my method. "My point is...I think that all beautiful creations, including sex, got distorted by, potentially, a mignon of the anti-Christ. Sex was made for intimacy, not for lust."

"So you're saying...?"

"Methinks you do question the inventor of the invention. I'm saying that you're holding on to some doctrine that says sex is a shameful, sordid activity. Perhaps you also gained a great identity about being the 'good girl,' about never putting a fingerprint out of place. Now you've been given all this new territory to go and play, and you're not sure where to start."

"I thought I was doing the right thing."

"You were, my love. But you also got religious and adhered to the right rules with the wrong motivation. I didn't expect to see you for at least the first six months because you'd be practicing the art of making love," I said, wondering if the penny had dropped.

She looked over at Petal, now suspended upside down on some fishing wire. Petal may not have been helping me here. I could practically hear Pats internally compare herself to Little Miss Private Dancer here.

"I'm not like these liberal woman who can embrace their sexuality. I'm a little trapped. I'm a little scared. I want to make him happy."

"You think Petal is feeling liberal?"

"Carrie, she gave not a care in the world as she just winked to the only man here, who just ignored her and asked us what could be a number nine across, ten letter word for 'a railway worker consuming fruit first, providing sustenance.' She looks pretty liberal to me." Her deflation was palpable.

"She was crying in the bathroom thirty minutes before her show because her boyfriend called her a whore on the telephone. She's seeking answers just like you and me."

Silence.

"I didn't notice how much I attached my purity to my identity or how much shame would occur when encouraged by God to have sex with my new husband."

Here I was, cleaning up my act, and yet a girl who had no act to clean was feeling more shame than I was. We had had different experiences, and by this point I was seeking what God really thought about our mistakes. If the devil wanted to ensure we didn't get intimacy, one effective method was to create shame about our sexuality.

It was something my non-Christian friends always brought up. "There's too much shame with you, Carrie. It's that religion you've been swallowing all these years. It's made a shame out of your perspective of sex," friends would say. "You need to loosen up."

I agree that often the Church has been ignorant of the reality of sexual desires. I agree that too much shame has been splurged onto the topic of sex in the hope that pre-marital adventures would be avoided. The joy of sex was dished out for the secular world to obtain, and the fear of sex was all that was left for those of us still sitting in the pews. So often we religiously shoved desires under the sea grass carpet because of shame. Renaissance art was still hidden in crypts of some churches to hide its nude drawings of the Christ, yet the same artwork was once suspended on the walls of cathedrals. This wasn't about self-mortification of the flesh or seeking pain in self-denial. Had the church become more frightened of the liberal world we were moving in? Is that why Renaissance art was now covered in cloth?

I concur with all of the accusations made toward a dated Church. Anything, even true things, can be distorted, and whether we were purer than cupid's puppy, or a little wild like me, shame always seemed to attach itself to our sexual (or non-sexual) histories. Whatever I had done, whatever *interesting* decision I made in the past, I had become so far removed from the old me, so unfamiliar to my old ways that when I recited stories of how I used to be, I talked in third person.

Since my last break up, I had moved to California for a new life. I was immersed in an environment where we were much more honest about our choices, and therefore became far more powerful. I was clean from self-sabotaging activities; I tried hard not to look back. I didn't repeat the same mistakes because I'd had a enough epiphanies to see that my sexual past wasn't working, not for me or my exes, not for the future "him," not for the future me. My head was up, I was walking boldly once more…until I overheard a conversation, a casual confession from a boy I was interested in: "I'd like to hopefully marry a virgin." I knew this statement didn't represent the entire perspective of single people in Northern California, but I heard it nevertheless.

How does one respond to such remarks? With such a stark contrast to the usual hedonistic world I had come from, what was I to do? Start jumping on tabletops, preaching the themes of redemption that filled the gospel? Accept that this was their preference, disregard their existence in church forevermore simply because their statement made me feel like a second-class citizen? Should I chime a bell to all of my fellow "redeemed" friends who took similar sexual paths and start a "born-again virgins" club? Or would I buy a one-way ticket to a place too many people ended up by the end of their twenties: Shameland. After I decided to become abstinent again, I now found myself dating men who had held onto their purity. Suddenly the question, "Am I *good* enough for him?" was a puzzle that needed solving. As conversations unveiled the truth, I learned that neither men nor women usually cared for your past as long as you carried no shame in the present.

Wishing to marry a virgin if you chose a life of purity yourself wasn't a bad thing; it's an understandable request, no different perhaps than me wanting a man who is taller than I am. I've equally noted some great potential I've missed because of this requirement that I held against those who were, let's say, more vertically challenged.

Knowing the pain of shame, I chose to embrace the decisions men made today in purity, not the mistakes they had overcome a long time ago. There were many men and women who had a colorful past; and some people had nothing more than monochrome in their relationship history. But when these worlds collided, it was easy for the former group, when facing a community of people who've been pure all their days, to let the scoundrel that is shame whisper bitter nothings in their ears and rob them of hope and a sense of worth.

Within minutes of hearing someone might want to marry a virgin, I nearly clothed myself in degradation, lowered my head a little more, and couldn't look anyone in the iris. Within the next few days, I'd forgotten my name, never mind my history with the Lord. One person's opinion, one person's ability to hold to their purity, somehow thwarted my recovery from mistakes I made in my past.

"Guilt says I've made a mistake. Shame says I am a mistake," Brené Brown once told a crowd during a TED Talk. [7] Through many conversations like the one with Pats and with Generation Z, those who felt they wouldn't be suitable for a man or woman who had led a fairly spotless sexual history, I realized just how debilitating shame was, how erosive, unproductive, pitiful, and victim-like it made the soul feel. Grace was introduced to take us to the dance floor and show us off, while shame was an entrapment tool used to make us believe we didn't deserve the best, welding us to the floor so we could not fly.

It took having a few male mates, gorgeous men who valued purity, placing me in front of a mirror, forcing me to look at myself while each one told me: "I refuse to hold your past against you." But still, for a period of time there was something within me refusing to let go of shame. It had become a comfort blanket, one that kept me from having to feel vulnerable by preventing me from sharing my past with someone who might just love me unconditionally. I carried it around because I felt I should in order to show how remorseful I was.

Life was too short to make my past mistakes, the ones I had already conquered, be resurrected. Faith told me to let it go; God said He had me covered. I never saw a snake return to its old skin, so why hold onto mine? Self-value couldn't come from a place of "what have you done?" but a place of "look how far you've come!" Shame did not enable me to repair anything, which only left me more hopeless. It encouraged me to settle for the same unhealthy, codependent relationships, constantly seeking for someone else to say, "You're OK."

Sometimes we carry shame because we don't risk at all. We have apologized. We have said our Hail Marys. We have sat in a confessional box for 300 hours as though it were community service. We have written letters to our victims and to ourselves. We have gone over the reasons why we did what we did. We have seen married men, after intense extra-marital affairs, carry webcams on their person so their wives would know where they were at all times. For the record, it wasn't her idea. It was his.

People push fear to the back burner, thinking they've moved on. I've come to believe that muffling emotions is what turns subconscious feelings into poisonous self-medication, harsh condemnation toward others, or a repetition of the same crime. Sex addicts weren't doing it *for* the thrill; they were doing it *from* the shame.

On the same trip to the Philippines I took back in 2013 to counsel rescued victims of sex-trafficking, an interpreter, a colleague, and I sat down with one seventeen-year-old girl, let's call her Clementine, who had been rescued from "the bars"—known as brothels to you and me.

She couldn't look me in the eyes.

"Are you ready?" I asked my interpreter.

"As ready as I'll ever be," she breathed deeply.

I looked to my teammate and told her to chip in at any point. We managed well on facial expressions and sign language throughout the hour. We began attempting eye contact as I spoke: "I need you to know a few things. Anything you tell me is received without judgment and in confidentiality as long as you aren't in current danger. If you are, I will need to tell those who look after you. We want to know your story and how you think we can help you. Is that okay?"

She nodded, paused, and then began to speak: "All right, here it is. I was selling my body until four weeks ago."

She was taking ownership; she wasn't playing victim, despite the
sexual abuse she had suffered from her family and the manipulation she
had faced in the brothels. She was feisty. And I liked it.

I wish I had lined my stomach beforehand, though, as I began to hear
the details of her story. She had been molested by her father, brothers,
uncles. Her mother fell ill, which ended in her living in a hospital. Her
father left. She had no education, no income, not enough food to feed her
siblings. So she grabbed a job at a bar through the introduction of one of
her friends. She began by waitressing, but because of the reputation of girls
who worked at those "bars," she was soon labeled a prostitute. Rejected
by her mother as a result, and with no education, she had no choice other
than to provide an "extra service" in the bar, starting at the age of fifteen.
As she told her story, my head began to swell, and my imagination got the
better of me.

No warning came to tell me it looked this ugly. Her tears fell all
over the place: on her jeans, on my dress, right into my own soul. Forget
Scandal. You want drama? It was right here, full of agony, disease, incest.
First impressions of my personal tale compared to hers told me we were
worlds apart in our perspectives. But in the corners of our minds, we
shared the same need: to fly in freedom.

"Shall I tell you what freedom looks like?" I whispered. She looked
into my eyes for the first time. "It looks like unchaining yourself from
the unforgiveness you have toward those who have caused you to suffer.
No more do you stay suffering in shame. It's time to get this pain out. I'm
giving you a journal so you can write it all down. No names, no locations
in case you lose it. Then burn it. You need to know your worth on this
planet. I need you to understand that what these people have done to you
is not acceptable; it is evil, it is dumbfounding—and they are broken. Only

you can decide you can be powerful and strong, a fighter for your own freedom and a force for good. You need to start forgiving these people—and yourself. You needn't ever see them again, but we need to help you leave the baggage behind. Otherwise, you'll stay in unhealthy relationships, believe you deserve abuse, and you'll judge everyone including yourself. You'll live in constant fear and hatred. And you're better than that. I know it."

I looked at her face, and on her right cheek she had a beauty mark. This rocked me because I had had a dream about a girl with a beauty spot on her right cheek two months before my trip. I'd been asking God to highlight people to me for this time in the Philippines. No wonder my soul felt so warm toward her.

I put the pen down. "I've just been reminded of something," I said to the interpreter. "I'm about to change the scheme of things here."

"Okay?"

"Tell her I was given a dream about her two months ago."

As she began to interpret my words, I saw Clementine's face begin to change. Written all over it was, "You mean I was in a plan? Before I even stopped selling my body?"

I carried on: "From all the things you have endured, all the things you faced, you will rescue a hundred times more girls than I ever could. You are meant to build bridges for hope and rescue the dying souls of the Philippines. The rebellion you showed at times against your family—that made you fight for your name—will continue, but this time it will be for freedom. You're a fighter, defiant to the end. You will not give up. You know the darkest side of man, and you can overcome it by saving many more like you. Do you understand how special you are? God has anointed you with an inner willpower that will not stumble, that will not be left on the floor."

The Philippines is a country built on shame culture; in no other place on Earth is it harder to escape it. But Clementine managed to. In a matter of days she had made a decision to go back to school and to become a freedom fighter. I think about her all the time because, before she was the age I lost my virginity, she had already overcome a level of shame that could have resided in her soul forever. Instead, she faced the pain and achieved something that few manage to in their entire lives.

Too many stories had confronted me, too many that ended in freedom. I knew I had to make a decision and work through my shame in order to be able to love myself fully. It would mean that fear would not invade my relationships, that I could be able to trust my discernment more. With my entire story being used for good, even Pats could see the meaning in shameless sex. She and I worked through that warfare, and it was warfare, but as we all know, love always wins in any battle. Within the next few months Patsy was liberated within herself for the first time, her walk a little more upbeat, and her husband smiling like a Cheshire cat from East London to Timbuktu.

It was watching this process that taught me that shame was as poisonous as cyanide. It cut off intimacy and brought fear in a 360-degree radius. By consciously declaring that God's love could disinfect shame, I began to walk with my head held upright. If a prostitute who endured such terrible torture could slowly brush off degradation and bathe herself in the forgiveness of God, then I, too, could eradicate the remnants of condemnation. I *could* learn to love again—this time to the fullest. It was going to take a little while to face all that I had been given by unhealthy guys, by allowing such to enter into my life. Most of my shame stemmed from questions surrounding why I had allowed my heart to be treated like a workbench. As I ensured I didn't repeat the same destructive behaviors, I also allowed myself to see how much I had overcome. This was my backbone, my standard. Purity attracts healthy thoughts, forgiveness seeks connection, humility invites love. The fear of the Lord was a vital and beautiful thing, but I never confused it with shame, never diluted it with misnomers that separated me from the intimacy that was waiting for me, dying for me, accepting me...

 ...for all that I am.

 ...for all that I was.

 ...for all that I could become.

CHAPTER 12

Worth the Wait?

I so often get asked, "You're a Christian, so what *don't* you do?" Is that all the Gospel is about to people outside of the Church? A bunch of rules? I'm the last person to submit to a list of guidelines if that is all God emulates. No. Those who are truly developed in spirituality choose not to have sex before marriage because it is a form of self-love, sacrificial love for someone else.

These fluffy descriptions from the Church about "saving ourselves," that we get too emotionally attached or "bite off more than we can chew" when we have sex before marriage are cringe-worthy sentiments that made most of the secular world, including myself, embarrassed about the Church's reasons for chastity. Yet, oddly enough, it was the science of sex that made me a believer in purity. Reputable scientists were beginning to see that neurons in the brain were rewired when we "made love" to anyone. And I mean *anyone*. The chemicals involved—dopamine, oxytocin, serotonin—I was learning, were created for a specific reason. They were in every brain, in every human to bond a mother to her child, to bond a man to a woman. So when I found my faith in the Essence, the Designer of the earth once more, and after years of witnessing the insatiable tears of girls who couldn't believe a boy didn't call them the morning after, I slowly began to trust that abstinence was actually fatherly advice rather than religious nonsense. If Christ told people that He came so that we could have joy and to its fullest, it was time for me to start listening to His advice on how to live. By embracing the concepts of faith, joy was exactly what I got in return, not a collection of miserable doctrines that made me more repressed.

But after that comes the number one question used to argue my abstinence, one I am so tired of hearing: "What if you wait until your wedding night, Carrie, and you two aren't sexually compatible?" The desire for sexual compatibility had created a lie that sensual harmony was either evident, or not. Like freckles, you either had them or you didn't.

In the years I played it pure, my naiveté, I confess, invented some incredible methods to decipher whether a potential future husband was going to be physical dynamite with me, a fear so ridiculous in hindsight. It didn't seem to matter if he had an addiction or the personality of a doorstop as long as he was great in the sack. My ridiculous assessments went something like this: Could he dance like Patrick Swayze without over-enthusiastic shoulders? How did he handle hardware tools? Was he nifty in a game of Twister? Was he blind? (Rumor had it that lack of eyesight meant he was pretty good with all other senses. I actually sought blind men out for a time. Okay, I didn't.) The questions were endless, and pointless.

I tested my instincts with bizarre theories because I was terrified of the possible negative consequences if I discovered on my wedding night, the first time I would make love to the one man I had held out for, that we were as compatible as a mongoose and a cobra. Of course, I heard horror stories of people waiting till their wedding night, saving themselves with quite the purity plan, divorcing a year or two later because someone's anatomy reminded them of a "thimble" or because their sex drives were completely bipolar. It's true, people do divorce, even Christians, because of sexual incompatibility.

Cut to a speaking engagement this past year that pointed out the *real* issue behind this fear, this idea about compatibility. I had just spoken to a women's group in London on the content of my first book. I talked about white knuckling, now at thirty-five and single, how my patience on some days is tough, knowing that sex is awesome, knowing the power of it, the connection in it, the breaking down of walls that skin-on-skin contact can do. The whole time I was secretly afraid that without a ring on my finger, I wouldn't be trusted by a group of women wanting to know if what I believed actually worked. I had no husband to wrap up the story, no relationship as such to say, "Choosing purity? Here's what you *do* win!" before cueing the entrance of a dashing Brazilian man with the brains of a neuroscientist and the emotional maturity of Saint Augustine. Not that it was on my requirement list, but it was what I thought women would want to see. Without a healthy relationship, how could I be an inspiration for others in this area?

After I spoke, I talked to many women, but I noticed one in particular waiting patiently. She was beautiful, in her forties with long dark hair, and had waited to talk to me for fifteen minutes. Finally, she had her chance. The other women surrounding us didn't give us much space, intrigued to see what I'd share with someone else on a different type of journey. I was impressed with her patience.

"I'm afraid I'm not sure I agree with you," she confessed.

"Okay?" I smiled, ready to take the punch.

"You see, I did all of this. I waited for marriage. I waited for the guy, and he did for me. Now I'm divorced after he had an affair. He's shacked up with someone else. All down to sexual incompatibility. How was I rewarded? I did everything right, and now I'm not so sure it works."

I could see why she wouldn't want to wait; I could see why "being righteous" had made her question everything when her world went down the pan.

"Can I ask a question?" I replied.

"You just did," she joked.

I laughed at her cockiness.

"Forgive me for asking things which I know you probably have tried, but for my reference and understanding, entertain me."

"Okay."

"How was counseling between you both?"

"He wouldn't go." She looked me right in the eyes.

The women were now intrigued with this confrontation about the most intimate parts of her broken relationship. A silence fell among all of us as she divulged that her husband wouldn't even seek advice for their marriage. She nearly broke in the stillness, no words could be found for such poor treatment.

"I'm sorry. And I'm speechless."

"So maybe this whole 'saving yourself' doesn't work for everyone. Maybe it isn't worth the wait?"

"I can see why you feel that hopeless, but you're missing one valid point," I interjected.

"What's that?"

The women surrounding us were now watching our dialogue like a tennis match.

"Saving sex doesn't mean you're going to have the most dynamite husband, nor even the best relationship. Holding out isn't like a workout where you expect a chiseled body at the end of it. All it's done for me as a single person is help me be more liberated, especially in regards to whom I choose to date and for how long."

"So what would you have learned in my experience?" She was asking with an open mind, not a wish to trample me down or berate me for speaking about purity. She generally wanted to learn, and so I felt at liberty to respond.

"The fact that he didn't go to counseling says to me that he doesn't have a curious mind nor a selfless heart, a mind that wishes to communicate nor a perspective to believe he could make this better. Did he act like a victim most of the time?"

"Yeah. Very much so."

"I'm afraid that's typical of someone who reacts to his choices, rather than takes charge. I'm not sad that you guys couldn't find sexual compatibility. I'm sad that he couldn't spend sixty minutes in a session with some humility to learn from someone who might have the capacity to have an objective point of view, or indeed accept that he is part of the equation as to why you guys weren't having awesome sex. You didn't split because of dynamite-less sex. You broke up because he wasn't willing to be in a team with you."

She fell to the floor.

All of us placed our hands on her in comfort as she curled into a ball. I talked into her ear of what she now had learned, that this wasn't the end, that it was just the beginning. A new journey to discover the self, never mind find a man who was willing to be on a team, to be kind and curious to learn, one who loved the Lord so much that he would never neglect, punish, nor abandon one of His daughters. She needed a man who would stand by the promise he made in front of a crowded room, who'd stay committed to the cause.

Prude: Misconceptions of a Neo-Virgin

The question of "What if you're not sexually compatible?" should never be the question. Shouldn't there be more to relationships than this anyway? The real question should be, "Do you like who you are? Are you loving yourself enough to therefore give it out, rather than constantly seeking from a massive vat of lack?" An emotional connection, an admiration for the other, teamwork, perhaps confrontation that doesn't involve being left to cry on the stairs? If the need for sexual gratification was taking over a man's love for me, then it was only a matter of time before one of us broke away, lied, found another person's love because we believed we had the right to be given whatever we wanted. When we don't have a real urge to sacrifice for our beloved, then we'll never want to work on the relationship, never mind chemistry.

It turned out I didn't need some Brazilian named Felipe to prove that choosing to have sex at a particular time in life was the only way forward. Too many have saved until marriage, and relationships have still fallen apart. Too many didn't save, yet the brilliance of continuous sex didn't always work for them either, resulting in shame, their future man not wanting to hear just how many other men his woman had been sexual with before him.

The circuitry in men and women was that we wanted to feel exclusive in the most intimate of relationships. We couldn't deny that. Many times I've seen men and women be rather proud of their promiscuous years only to feel disturbed when they finally met their match. Once they found the person they wanted to share life with, they wished they had saved something special for him or her. Emotional maturity brings regret, despite societal or cultural expectations. Rather, it was our inner wiring that made me fully believe sex was only invented to fuse two people together who were meant to stay together—for life.

As one married friend shared with me, "Sexual compatibility is only an issue if you have a self-centered view of sex, more focused on what satisfies you and grading people as to how well they do that. If you have a selfless, giving attitude to sex, compatibility issues dissipate as sex becomes a quest to discover and please your partner—with them hopefully doing likewise. This is the key to a loving and ever-improving sex life."

I realized that if my future husband and I wait for intimacy until we are in covenant, our wedding night would most likely be a three-second wonder, especially if he has held out beforehand. Any other hope would be like expecting him to have the muscular structure of The Rock by lifting 15lb weights for one night only. As my friends who had waited told me, "It was in the training." For many of them, that first year of marriage was quite the laboratory of sexual exploration. The key was that they were seeking to please each other, not themselves.

For all the couples that weren't making it, the ones who broke up or, worse yet, divorced, rarely did it come down to bedroom antics. More marriages were struggling with communication (followed by disconnection and dishonesty) than sexual incompatibility. Sex often stopped if spouses didn't have an emotional reason to be vulnerable. If there were some couples that connected on all levels but struggled in the compatibility department, then sex therapy was at hand—and it worked for my friends, as long as they wanted it to.

As I've watched more friends divorce, half the time it appeared they had no clue what they were signing up for in marriage until they lived with each other. In the past my parents counseled more people in their first year of marriage than at any other point. Bring kids into the equation and, oh mama, you had to make sex work on a whole new schedule.

Being intensely intimate with everyone we might like wasn't only disintegrating the exclusivity in every date we encountered, but it also began to build up more walls when it came to the "free for all" perspective.

As soon as we believed we didn't have to work for something, that we didn't have to be patient, to fight for, to focus, to communicate, to value, to honor, to cherish another human being, then we were able to place our own sexual desires first, to "get laid loads," to fulfill physical urges while stamping on emotional requirements in another human being.

That's not love. That's greed.

Of course, all of this is nice to the ears but hard to believe. We can't envision decent relationships or healthy dating if it's not around us, and in all honesty, I didn't discover much health even within the Church until I flew to California. Did London harbor poor management of relationships? Not at all. Some were beautiful to watch. But for many, purity had become just another wall to keep people out. There was just as much codependency or too much fear of intimacy in the Church as outside of it.

It wasn't an intended dream of mine to live in a place that valued purity almost as much as oxygen, it just sort of fell upon me in the circumstance of watching revival take place in a particular church. Did revival occur from purity? Not necessarily. Did purity bring you a happier marriage and 2.4 children and a white picket fence, allowing you to spend your mornings in an Anthropologie apron, baking bread? No.

Perhaps I was fortunate on some level because despite my faithless relationships, I was surrounded by people who did save themselves and had built a foundation of trust, emotional connection, teamwork, respect with an addition of humor on the topic of sex. I needed to surround myself with honest married couples, ones who, after a decade of marriage with four or five kids under their belt, would retell their wedding night as comedy material for the dinner table. Needless to say, their terrible first attempts brought tears to my eyes and had me choking on my Pellegrino. I learned that for people who actually worked through this stuff, the foundation of their marriage was honesty and *talking*. Terrible sex, incompatible sex could turn into something quite peachy, but the majority of relationships didn't stay around to watch the change.

I wasn't waiting for some fantastic results thanks to my own self-discipline in my single years. Living by the wisdom God had given was never given for us simply to avoid God's eternal damnation. It was always *for* His children, given to us with kindness. I was waiting because I didn't need to stay in unhealthy relationships. I was waiting because I believed in what really bonded me to men outside of sex: communication, selflessness, a union of pleasure and fun outside of rubbing sexual parts together. Oh, I know how connected you can feel in sex; I know how vulnerable it can be, but sex isn't really all that dynamite when you know the man can (and will) leave you when he's done. It's not so great when you know the man has placed his own gratification and desire in front of yours. There is an intimacy that only really comes with lifelong vows and a "I'm doing this with you to the end" mentality, and *that* is what knocks sex right off its sub-pleasurable state and right into the stratosphere. It's the kind of sex I've heard of, but yet to experience.

After having men in my life who refused to leave fingerprints on me until I was all theirs, ones who challenged me to push deeper into a relationship with God before a relationship with them, who wanted to fight for my growth over their sexual desires, I noticed a startling difference between them and the exes I would occasionally catch up with who were still living sexual lifestyles. The contrast almost turned my stomach. They still lived in a realm of "me, me, me." They still invited women back to their apartments without any thought for tomorrow. These were the ones you could guarantee would throw away a counselor's phone number. These were the relationships where men and women were too scared to share their needs, to share their hurt over something said, or to have a voice in the relationship for fear they'd be left, abandoned, or wreck their Facebook relationship status in one fell swoop because she told him he didn't treat her very well in front of others that evening.

There is the flipside. We all know of people (I have many friends like this) who found awesome partners and had sex well before the mention of marriage. They represent the majority of Western civilization, and it's worked for them. Some did make it down the aisle, and I've been there celebrating those unions. I was delighted they made it because many don't. Those success stories haven't been the most common. The majority of people do end up having a fair few sexual partners before meeting "the one," and more often than not, those relationships weren't the happiest of endings. Perhaps they were like me and were too merciful to men based on their words while their actions weren't following through to real commitment. Maybe they were attracted to the unavailable type; maybe they were one of the forty million women in the U.S. who are classified as "codependent." Maybe they simply wanted to be loved and thought that sex would finally bring that connection.

My revelation was that real love doesn't require sex to initiate it. Sex is just a beautiful by-product, an important bonding tool on days when marriage is tough. I didn't choose the lifestyle because I had had some uncomfortable moments with men; their treatment didn't frighten me into celibacy. Far from it. I found that when things weren't going well with a man, the desire to keep our hands off each other was almost impossible. We wanted to connect to make things better, and often the physical was the last resort in a rough relationship. When I entered into healthier ones, the urge to listen before touching, to look before feeling, to give before taking led me into a much better understanding of even my faith.

My lack of prudishness, my openness and honesty about sex, made me feel clean without coming across as too sterile. When it came to tolerating poor behavior from a man who wanted to have me in his life to make himself feel better rather than to form a union with me to do radical things in the world, I chose to not enter into the relationship, refusing to adhere to the "let's see how it goes" sentiment. Any man in my life using the possibility of incompatibility as a reason to have sex before marriage was only worth sending a greeting basket as I retired from the relationship, skipping to my heart's content. I didn't want to be manipulated with ultimatums or fear. If he really couldn't do a relationship without sex before marriage, I would simply applaud his honesty and let him go.

My friendships, my family, my colleagues, my teams, my men, and my girls bring me such joy in my life that I can't go back now. I'm too free, too aware of what is good for me, too in touch with God's heart to want to purposefully hurt it. After everything was said and done in my life—with my father, my exes, my friends, and my faith—connection was always a necessity. But connection for me now is fulfilled in measures that my culture has forgotten: a smile from a friend on a rough day; a sweet note left for me from my intern in the book I was reading; turning up to a meeting and finding someone has left my favorite kombucha in my seat; the man who packed my bag and whisked me away to Napa for the weekend to the vineyard that makes my chosen wine; the man who defended my name when I wasn't around, even when I'd hurt him; the friend who celebrated my success when hers was falling apart; the man who wanted us to wait because he was *just that into me.*

We want dynamite and expect to find it in a hot night with some guy. Dynamite, for me anyway, was discovered in loving past myself, past my expectations, and when I left religious doctrine and isolating judgment (the church's or secular world's slamming of my personal life decisions) out in the cold to die. I found it in the permission to be vulnerable, for this was the only place I could ever fully be myself. Today the world is so focused on being ruthless, being hard-nosed, having sexual encounters without letting emotions get involved, being ready to walk away without a need to feel anything. That isn't the life that screams, "You're free!" That life actually trapped me into believing I was powerless in my relationships with men and in my life decisions.

Amid all my tales, from begging a man to wait to begging a man to drive for fifteen minutes, from forgiving my father to forgiving myself, from my atheistic arrogance to my desire to emulate Christ, all I wanted at day's end was to know I made healthy choices in an unhealthy world, to know I gave more than I took, that I caused more good than harm.

Despite how misinterpreted faith is in the modern world, whether it's a thwarted lens through the documentaries of extreme fundamentalists or a Christian on a street corner condemning every passer-by through a speakerphone, my personal experience—the comforting encounters, the ones that dismantled my own self-sabotage—were real to me. The joy from self-love had to be carried out by getting outside of myself, finding a greater power, a kinder power. The journey of the relationship between me and the complexity of God was broken down into a relationship that could be interpreted into human understanding. Faith is so much greater, so much holier than the words on the page.

The identity that I had grasped in my own performance to match the world didn't work. My maturity came only when I decided to be a kid, a child, a daughter to the arbiter of the Universe. My connection with "Him" formed a heart in me that still wanted to listen even if someone shouted at me, that wanted to reach out when the other pushed away.

And when it came to sex, the most intimate action any two human beings could do together, I wanted it to be worth the fight, the patience, the exclusivity, the diamond in the rough. Just like it was in the 1940s, when people prided themselves in focusing on one person, rather than left and right swipes from a Tinder application on their smartphones. If we embraced our Father's advice, wouldn't the world become a little less fearful of abandonment, with fewer walls to cover vulnerability, become, once again, a little more secure, a little more family orientated, a little more in love?

For none of this journey was a case for self-love so much as a case for humanity.

The End.

Endnotes

[1] Joe S. Mcllhaney Jr. M.D. and Freda McKissic Bush M.D., *Hooked: New Science on How Casual Sex Is Affecting Our Children*, (Chicago: Moody Publishers, 2008). Used with permission.

[2] Scott Christian, "Ten Reasons Why You Should Quit Watching Porn," *GQ*, November 20, 2013, www.gq.com/story/10-reasons-why-you-should-quit-watching-porn (accessed September 1, 2015).

[3] Allison Pearson, "Pornography has Changed the Landscape of Adolescence Beyond all Recognition," *The Telegraph*, April 22, 2015, www.telegraph.co.uk/women/mother-tongue/11554595/Pornography-has-changed-the-landscape-of-adolescence-beyond-all-recognition.html (accessed September 1, 2015). Used with permission.

[4] Louis Theroux, *Louis Theroux: Twilight of the Porn Stars*, directed by Jason Massot (2012; United Kingdom: British Broadcasting Corporation), film.

[5] "The F Word: Stories of Forgiveness Exhibition," *The Forgiveness Project*. (2005). www.theforgivenessproject.com/programmes/exhibition/ (accessed September 1, 2015).

[6] Brené Brown, "Listening to Shame," TED2012, www.ted.com/talks/brene_brown_listening_to_shame?language=en (accessed September 1, 2015).

Acknowledgements

The Red Arrow Team

Vanessa Chandler—for running the race against all the odds, for your belief in my voice enough to fight for it to be heard this side of the great pond. Signing on the dotted line has never been more fun, nor as delicious in bubbles and chocolate. Here's to you, your journey and all that is to come. Thank you for the faith you've had in Him and therefore in me. Your eye for detail and heart for excellence is second to none.

Jennifer Westbrook—from those beautiful nights at C.S Lewis' house and the words that emanated from his desk. You helped shape and structure my voice into a comprehensive format. America may still not know what a "pipette" is, and perhaps that is no bad thing. What a gift you have been to me, a gift I shall talk about for many years to come. Thank you for all of it, beginning, middle and end.

Megan Cotton—you saw it all from the beginning, and how delightful it is to now have you work with me on Prude. Thank you for your tireless work, your beautiful ideas, your friendship through the stories even in this book, and your activating heart. It's contagious and I want a crate of it. This will not be the last book your name is mentioned in.

Sarah Harris—your voice and perspective were so valuable in this journey. I couldn't have taken the stance I did without it. You helped merge the worlds I've lived in, and created it into a real world. Thank you.

Organizations

Bethel Church—my heartfelt thanks to the father of Bethel, and the voice of reason in all things writing, Pastor Bill Johnson. Your kindness is as perennial as the grass and your voice will forever leave an imprint in my choice to write. My life is not the same now you're in it—and I'm quite okay with that.

Pastor Hayley Braun—the light in my day and the woman who covers my back. This year has been a platinum experience because of your teamwork with me. Thank you.

My interns—Joshua Ainsworth, Ashley Crandall, Trevor Derr, Benjamin Friedemann, Abigail Wardle—your love for me has blown me away, I could not have dreamed of a finer team than you. I've said it before, but thank you for choosing to love me, before you even knew my name.

Moral Revolution—for helping make this book PG.

C.S. Lewis Foundation—for allowing me to reside in Jack's house during the summer of 2015. What revelation and joy it was to stay in his home, amid the attic to the Narnia manuscripts. Thank you for the hospitality and all that those nights spent there gave me.

Family

My father, Pops—for the value you poured into me, for the honesty in when you couldn't, and for teaching me the heart of Christ amid the dark and the light. I miss you every day and none of this would be possible without your love and laughter. Until Heaven pops, until Heaven…

My mother, Mamma May, Mrs Tiggywinkles—for trusting me in all that I do, in all that I write. Your willingness to share me with America renders me breathless. As a great carrier of peace, you set a standard that keeps friendship and relationships stable in my life. How wonderful it is to say that the greatest person I know is also my mother. I love you. And that fluff-ball Nico.

My Deus, my light, my everything—look how far we have come? Look how glorious life became when I asked you to dream into my life again. Thank you for the blessings you've given to my life, for the light that is to come. I never want to write without you, I never want my heartbeat to leave your side. Here's to your desire for peace, for love, for light and for joy once more.

Carrie Lloyd is a professional writer and pastor. She has written about everything from fashion to faith for *Glamour*, *Magnify*, *Grazia*, *Company*, and *The Huffington Post*, and spoken about modern sex and love worldwide, as well as on television, radio and schools throughout the UK. Originally from London, Carrie currently resides in Redding, California, where she has completed ministry training and works at Bethel Church.

carrielloyd.org
herglassslipper.co.uk